Vietnam Scrapbook: an Army Pilot's Combat Tour

By Bob Steinbrunn

Cover Art By Don Greer

Squadron/Signal Publications

Author's Note

I wrote this book for a number of reasons. One was to leave a legacy for my children. In time, they will want to know more about what their dad did in the war. I thought it would be a shame if these photographs faded away like the pilot who took them, never to be preserved for future, more inquisitive generations. Perhaps the most compelling reason I wrote this book was to attempt to openly answer the question I received countless times during the past 40 years: What was it like to be a helicopter pilot in Vietnam?

I gave a straight answer to only a select few, the cognoscenti who have served there. The lifestyle we lived and the duties we performed were so alien to the average American civilian that it was generally a waste of time to attempt to take them into your mind, your remembrances, your heart. Civilians had no frame of reference, no similarities, no requirement to make sacrifices on a daily basis. They had no experience holding Death's hand for a year of combat.

Consequently, most Vietnam veterans returned home and led full and productive lives. However, they did so quietly. Few would talk about a place and a time to those who had no comprehension and little understanding. Further, those were turbulent national times. The war was unpopular, and the press and media were eager to report negatively on it. The nation reviled and shunned its servicemen and women, and the public acted like they wanted to forget the war and those who served in it.

Times have changed. The wounds have mostly healed and people, especially those born long after these events came to an abrupt conclusion, want to know. This small effort on my part attempts to address that curiosity, to present what it was like to be a combat helicopter pilot, to share the sights, the aircraft, the missions, and what we did in-between. We were soldiers once, and we were young. I would like you to know more about that.

Acknowledgments

Thanks to an editor friend for all his sage advice, help, and unending patience during my epic struggle with this first book.

Thanks to current Squadron/Signal authors and longtime friends Terry Love and Jim Goodall for providing recon and for illuminating the Landing Zone.

I took all photographs for this book. I captured many images under the press of combat. Thus, I beg the reader's indulgence for any photos that are less than optimal.

Dedication

To the air crew members, the aviation mechanics, and the armorers of A Troop, 7th Squadron, 17th Air Cavalry, who wrote history during the course of fighting an unpopular war in the Central Highlands of Vietnam. Gentlemen, you were superb, and I salute you. I was proud to have stood among you.

To the same personnel who made up the 189th Assault Helicopter Company, the "Ghostriders." They also delivered their very best in the mountains of Vietnam. When my call sign was "Ghostrider 22," I felt privileged to be a part of you. You were remarkable.

ISBN 978-0-89747-565-5

Military/Combat Photographs

If you have any photos of aircraft, armor, soldiers, or ships of any nation, particularly wartime snapshots, why not share them with us and help make Squadron/Signal's books all the more interesting and complete in the future? Any photograph sent to us will be copied and returned. Electronic images are preferred. The donor will be fully credited for any photos used. Please send them to:

Squadron/Signal Publications
1115 Crowley Drive, Carrollton, TX 75006-1312 U.S.A.
www.SquadronSignalPublications.com

About the Special Series

Squadron/Signal Publications' most open-ended genre of books, our Special category features a myriad of subjects that include unit histories, military campaigns, aircraft, ships, armor, and uniforms. Upcoming subjects include war heroes and non-military areas of interest.

If you have an idea for a book or are interested in authoring one, please let us know.

(Front Cover) ***September 1968.*** **"Barbie," a Bell UH-1H, heads home after an evening resupply mission to an artillery fire base in the Central Highlands of Vietnam. Barbie was assigned to me when I was part of Scarlet Lift Platoon, 189th Assault Helicopter Company, 52nd Combat Aviation Battalion at Camp Holloway, Pleiku.**

(Back Cover) A Bell UH-1C Iroquois "Huey" flies over the Central Highlands in Vietnam. This Huey (serial 66-649) had an XM-5 Weapons Subsystem and was part of Alpha Troop, 7th Squadron, 17th Air Cavalry Regiment (Air), 1st Aviation Brigade, Pleiku in May 1968.

(Preceding Page) A Hughes OH-6A from A Troop, 7th Squadron, 17th Air Cavalry, at readiness at Ban Me Thuot in the Central Highlands, 24 March 1968. Warrant Officers Don Peters and Frank Sheperis gaze at the camera. The aircraft's observer has protected the muzzle of his M-16 from grit with one of his flight gloves, posed to make a statement.

Introduction: The Army Aviation Pipeline

In January 1966, I entered the U.S. Army for four memorable years. My first assignment sent me to Fort Polk, Louisiana, for two months of basic combat infantry training where I learned the essentials of being a soldier. I learned about weapons, marksmanship, uniforms, marching, hand-to-hand combat, field tactics, the Uniform Code of Military Justice, and the proper care and polishing of combat boots.

The aviation pipeline next took me to the U.S. Army Primary Helicopter School at Fort Wolters, Texas, for eight months of preflight, primary, and advanced flight training. Fort Wolters' environment was similar to Officer Candidate School (OCS), where I trained to be an officer and a pilot. I took academic classes for half the day and flight training for the other half. While at helicopter school, I flew the Hiller OH-23 Raven.

The next stage took me to the U.S. Army Aviation Center at Fort Rucker, Alabama, for four months. There, I received two months of basic and advanced instrument training in the Bell TH-13T Sioux helicopter. This helicopter had the full instrument panel of a Bell UH-1 Iroquois ("Huey") and was an excellent instrument trainer. Next, I took the Huey transition course, which lasted one month. I flew several variants of the Huey that included the UH-1A, B, and D models. I then received training in tactics, formation flying, gunnery, external sling loads, field problems, and escape and evasion. Finally, after over a year in training, I graduated as an Army Aviator and officer. I had a technical rank of Warrant Officer 1 (WO-1), and I had approximately 210 hours of flight time.

Godman Army Airfield, Ft. Knox, Kentucky, June 1967. **(7th Squadron, 17th Air Cavalry Regiment) This insignia is on the nose of a Bell UH-1C Huey gunship and was painted on the compartment door using stencils. The insignia represents the spur (white) of the cavalry superimposed by a bolt of lighting (yellow), which denotes speed. The bolt lies on top of the spur at the upper right and passes under the spur at the lower left.**

United States Armor Center, Ft. Knox, Kentucky. **I wore this patch on the left shoulder of my uniform during the six months I trained at Ft. Knox. This patch denoted my current assignment or parent organization. The symbolism on the patch breaks down into yellow standing for the cavalry, red standing for the artillery, and blue standing for the infantry. In early World War II, armor became a separate branch and incorporated the three colors of the branches of the army, which were the armor's heritage. A symbolic tank track is superimposed by the barrel of a cannon. A lightning bolt is placed over the cannon.**

After graduation, the first alphabetical half of my class (about 150 pilots) was assigned directly to Vietnam as replacements for combat losses and for pilots who were rotating back to the States. The second alphabetical half of my class was sent to new units forming stateside, which would then be deployed overseas. In my case, I was fortunate enough to be sent to Fort Knox, Kentucky, where my new unit was forming at Godman Army Airfield. I was assigned to A Troop, 7th Squadron, 17th Air Cavalry "Ruthless Riders" as a pilot flying the short-cabin Bell UH-1C gunship.

Both the 3rd and 7th Squadrons of the 17th Air Cavalry formed at Fort Knox during the six months we were there, and we kept busy honing the skills we needed to function as a reconnaissance outfit. We trained to become the "eyes and ears" of the 4th Infantry Division, which was based at Camp Enari, Pleiku, in the Central Highlands of Vietnam. The six months we spent at Fort Knox were priceless in terms of us gaining additional experience and flight time. This experience would help us later on during combat.

After the unit was formed and deemed ready for war, we ferried the aircraft en masse from Fort Knox out to Sharpe Army Depot in Stockton, California. There, the aircraft were preserved and cocooned in a latex wrap and placed aboard the vintage World War II escort carrier USS *Breton*, a designated aircraft transport during Vietnam, for shipment overseas. My unit personnel boarded the USNS *General Nelson M. Walker*, a troop ship, at Oakland Naval Base, California, for the three-week voyage to Vietnam by way of Subic Bay in the Philippines.

The Overseas Movement

Hueys need to refuel about every two hours, so frequent stops were necessary for us to make the trip to California from Kentucky. Our legs on this flight were from Godman Army Airfield in Ft. Knox, Kentucky, to Campbell Army Airfield in Ft. Campbell, Kentucky, to Memphis Naval Air Station (NAS) in Memphis, Tennessee, to Texarkana Municipal Airport in Texarkana, Texas, to Dallas NAS in Dallas, Texas (5.5 flight hours), where we Remained Overnight (RON).

The next day's itinerary took us to Dyess Air Force Base (AFB) in Abilene, Texas, to Webb AFB in Big Spring, Texas, to Carlsbad Municipal Airport in Carlsbad, New Mexico, to Biggs Army Airfield in Ft. Bliss at El Paso, Texas (5.3 flight hours), where we had our second RON.

I consider the vastness of the Pacific Ocean.

29 August 1967. **I, a WO-1, stand with a Huey, Bell UH-1C on the ramp at Ft. Campbell, Kentucky, during the ferry flight to California.**

The third day took us to Libby Army Airfield in Ft. Huachuca, Arizona, to Phoenix Sky Harbor Airport in Phoenix, Arizona, to Yuma Marine Corps Air Station (MCAS) in Yuma, Arizona, to Palm Springs International Airport in Palm Springs, California, to Bakersfield Municipal Airport in Bakersfield, California (7.3) flight hours, where we had our third RON.

After returning to Ft. Knox to pack, we left several weeks later for Oakland Naval Base where we boarded the vintage 1945 USNS *General Nelson M. Walker*, a troop ship, for the voyage to Vietnam. We stayed on board for about a day and a half before we sailed early in the evening, which followed some arcane military custom. This time was the most poignant part of day—right at sunset, past San Francisco, under the glittering Golden Gate Bridge, and out into the broad reaches of the Pacific. As the still-glittering bridge passed below the horizon, I did not see one dry eye on board.

The voyage was a rolling and pitching one for three days until we passed off the Continental Shelf. Then, the ride was smooth and stable for the next 18 days. Without aircraft, the air crews ate, slept, read, played bingo, explored the ship, and played poker. I saw large amounts of money change hands during the cruise, and I was secretly glad I did not play.

Eventually, we drew up to the island of Luzon in the Philippines. We entered Subic Bay and moored for a day at the large naval base, where we reprovisioned. We spent a night at the Officer's club ashore, which most of us do not want to remember. However, we think the Navy will never forget.

After a morning departure, an easy two-day cruise brought us to Qui Nhon Harbor in (the former Republic of South) Vietnam. We unloaded at the harbor into 6 x 6 "deuce and a half" trucks for the long drive from Qui Nhon to Pleiku on Highway 19, where we passed through An Khe, the base location of the 1st Air Cavalry Division. The drive took forever, especially when we drove through the Mang Yang Pass where the French Group Mobile 100 was ambushed and slaughtered by the Viet Minh so many years before.

October 1967. **Troops line the bulwarks on board the USNS *General Nelson M. Walker* at pier side in the Oakland Naval Base in California.**

Camp Enari, Pleiku: 4th Infantry Division Home

Camp Enari, situated at the base of Dragon Mountain, was the base camp of the 4th Infantry "Ivy" Division, and we were invited to set up camp just inside the perimeter defenses. We erected General Purpose (GP) Medium tents. Each tent accommodated twelve pilots, their cots, sleeping bags, flight gear, and weapons. These tents, called "hooches" in GI vernacular, had wooden floors raised about two feet off the ground to distance them from predatory reptiles and insects. The side flaps opened for light and ventilation. While these accommodations were not five-star, they certainly beat living in a foxhole.

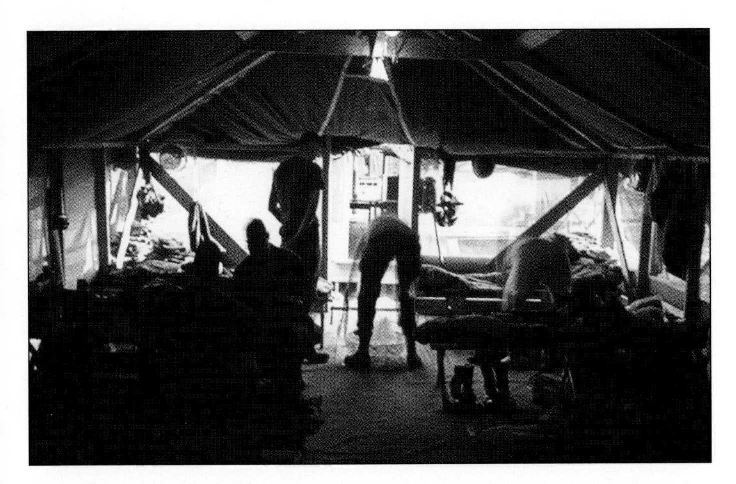

The inside of a GP Medium tent accommodated 12 pilots, their cots, gear, and weapons. The canvas sides rolled up for ventilation and light.

After the first mortar attack by elements of the North Vietnamese Army (NVA), the Ivy Division decided the hooches, however lavish, did not provide the level of protection we wanted. We decided to dig slit trenches outside the hooches and facing the perimeter wire about one hundred meters away. That way, we could seek shelter and brandish our .38 caliber Smith & Wesson revolvers at the enemy. The slit trenches were covered with boards, then with sandbags that absorbed shrapnel and other potentially lethal missiles. We hoped that one well-placed NVA mortar round would not land on top of and penetrate any of our trenches. Otherwise, a large group of expensively trained helicopter pilots might be neutralized.

We found out our opposition consisted of units of well-equipped, regular NVA troops rather than Viet Cong insurgents. Additionally, we learned that the NVA's weaponry was on a par with ours. This information made us reconsider the lethality of our .38 caliber revolvers.

Pilots, who were also officers, were not expected to do their own laundry or polish their own boots. We received permission to hire civilian Vietnamese females to come into camp for this purpose. For about a quarter per pilot, per day, each "hooch maid" washed and ironed 12 sets of jungle fatigues, polished 12 pair of boots, and made up 12 cots while we flew our missions. The hooch maids also felt free to sample any bags of potato chips, Cheesits, or other consumables they found. However, the women refused to eat our C-Rations. We took this refusal as some sort of culinary statement.

Pilots dig trenches covered with sandbags to serve as protective shelters during mortar attacks by the NVA.

Base Camp Defenses

The NVA were not the only unwelcome nocturnal visitors to Camp Enari. Multiple layers of defenses existed that made us feel somewhat less apprehensive about our hooches being located up against the perimeter. A number of infantry, armor, mortar, and artillery units provided defense in depth. Most of them had little appreciation for our requirement of a restful night's sleep.

Camp Enari's perimeter was ringed with guard towers that bristled with M60 machine guns, multiple layers of concertina barbed wire, Claymore mines, and tin cans tied to the wire that, hopefully, would alert the guards to an intruder's unwelcome presence. Despite all these defenses, NVA units breached our perimeter on numerous occasions, and our sleep was interrupted while we headed for our slit trenches with our weapons.

On several occasions, the NVA attacked us at night, and we spent the dark hours watching Douglas AC-47 "Spooky" gunships fire solid streams of tracer rounds into the perimeter wire as they circled the base camp. These valiant crews quickly responded to calls for help since they were located about five kilometers away at Pleiku Air

Vietnamese female civilians, our hooch maids, do laundry using foot power, aluminum bowls, and detergent while they enjoy the sunshine.

An engineer unit's M48 Armored Vehicle Launched Bridge (AVLB) is ready for action at Camp Enari.

(Above) The crew of an M88 "Hercules" Tracked Recovery Vehicle (VTR) wave and holler as they pass by our living area on the perimeter road. The primary use of the Hercules is tank recovery, and the Hercules weight (approximately 60 tons) makes our hooches shake when it rolls by.

Base, a joint United States Air Force (USAF) and Vietnam Air Force (VNAF) installation.

Even the daylight hours were not free from certain concerns while troops traveled outside the base camp. On one occasion, several NVA troops appeared on the side of the road when one of our ground infantry unit lieutenants, from the 7th squadron, D troop, drove the main road from Camp Enari to the city of Pleiku, which was located only three kilometers away. The NVA troops fired a Rocket Propelled Grenade (RPG) round at his Ford M151 "Mutt." An RPG was a weapon much like the American "Bazooka" but perhaps more lethal. The lieutenant's Mutt was a total write-off, and the Mutt's occupants escaped alive but with major injuries.

As an aside, model numbers and official names are assigned to military hardware, but the troops are the ones who properly name these items for posterity. For example, the official name for the "Huey" is actually a Bell Iroquois. In the incident just described, we always knew the Ford 151 "Mutt" as a "Jeep," and a Jeep, the Mutt shall remain.

(Above) An M113 Armored Cavalry Assault Vehicle (ACAV) of Pleiku Sector Area Command receives a mascot.

(Bottom Left) A U.S. troop holds a dead Royal Bengal tiger. The tiger became a casualty when the Scout Platoon found it from aloft in their Loaches.

(Bottom Right) A 4.2 inch, 1951 model mortar is in place as part of Camp Enari's Mortar Battery. This 649-pound weapon can throw out a 25-pound mortar round 5,297 yards.

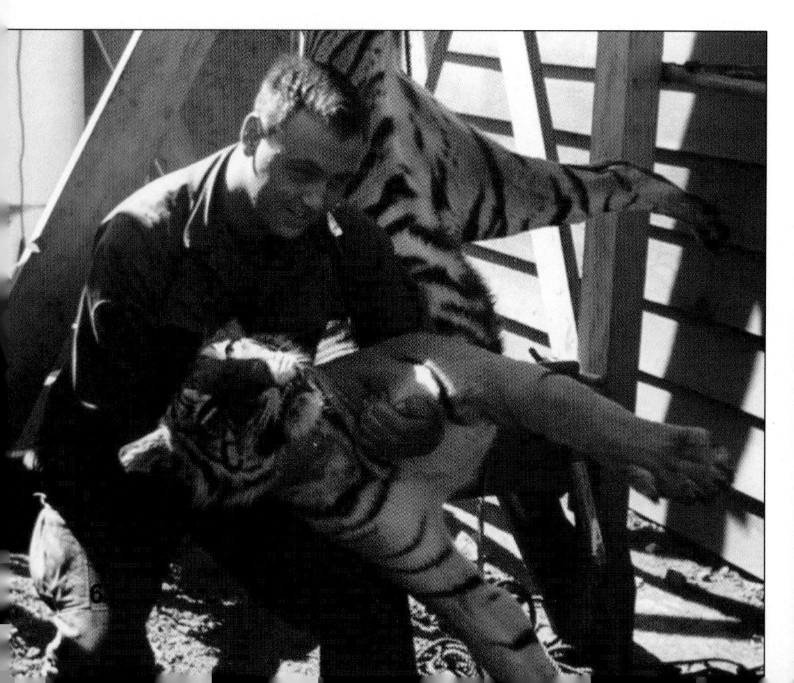

(Top Left) A mortarman holds the 25-pound round that shows the tan square wafers of propellant on the base. The range this explosive can be tossed is adjusted by adding or subtracting these wafers.

(Top Right) An M101, 105 mm howitzer is ready to fire high explosive (HE) rounds or flares during night attacks. This battery is not situated too close to us. It is located about an eighth of a mile away, but the noise this battery makes is still loud enough to wake the soundest sleeper. The noise aside, the mere fact this unit is firing means a good possibility exists that we need to head for the slit trenches.

(Bottom) An M151 Ford "Mutt" lies in the aftermath of being hit by a RPG, a bazooka-like weapon.

This 105 mm howitzer is put in place to fire a full 360 degrees since the artillerymen never know from what direction the next attack will come. Dragon Mountain looms faintly in the distance.

"Ruthless Riders" Build Helicopter Revetment Area

The 4th Infantry Division allocated space on the east side of the base camp for A Troop, B Troop, and Headquarters Troop to build the much-needed aircraft revetments; petroleum, oil, and lubricants (POL) refueling spot; and maintenance base necessary to operate aircraft. This area was located to the northeast of the main base camp's east–west runway of Hensel Airfield. We erected parking revetments here to protect the helicopters from blast fragments and other damage during mortar attacks. If one aircraft was destroyed during an attack, the revetment was designed to protect adjacent aircraft from being damaged by the resulting explosion from the destroyed aircraft.

The revetment had two parallel, lumber walls that were filled with dirt. The revetments were built wide enough to accommodate a gunship with its external armament. On windy days, taps on a revetment wall from a ship's Miniguns were not uncommon as the aircraft hovered in. This inadvertent contact caused damage to the gun, mount, or airframe. We considered this damage shameful. With gusty winds or a crosswind, landing outside the revetment was safer and easier. We then dragged the ship straight in by using enough power or torque to move the aircraft but not enough to break ground contact. This maneuver provided adequate directional stability to the helicopter so it would track straight into place between the revetment walls without contacting them. This superior pilot's technique was called cheating.

The ever-present red dust of Vietnam's Central Highlands permeated everything and was a hazard to flight operations and hovering helicopters. This dust restricted visibility. Its abrasiveness caused premature wear and failure on turbine engines when they ingested it. The red dust caked up on guns, ammunition feed chutes, optical sights, and rocket tubes. Winds blew the dust into open fuel tank filler necks during refueling, which clogged fuel filters or caused engine failure. One method of alleviating this hazard consisted of frequently spraying a black, tar-like substance called Peneprime on the ground. Spraying Peneprine provided a good temporary solution. Rotor wash and dragging helicopter skids meant frequent applications were needed to keep the dust down to a tolerable level. All our C-models had particle separators, which worked like a fancy air filter, installed later as kits. The particle separators fit over the engine intake plenum to provide better filtration.

This ammunition bunker sits alongside a revetment and contains crates of 7.62 mm linked ammunition for the Miniguns and M60 door guns. Cardboard tubes containing the 2.75 inch Folding Fin Aerial Rocket (FFAR) warheads and rocket motors are stacked inside. These two rocket components are screwed together by hand and then loaded into the aircraft's two M158 launchers.

(Above) An A Troop, 7th Squadron, 17th Cavalry Bell UH-1H "slick" (smooth and devoid of external armament) hovers over the revetment area's Peneprime surface. The revetments were built to protect each aircraft from mortar fragments as well as adjacent aircraft in the event one exploded from being hit. The revetment's design is intended to contain the blast to the immediate area. This view is to the west where Dragon Mountain shows up brightly in the morning sunlight in the distance.

(Below) A UH-1C with the XM-21 weapons sub-system lurks in its revetment. The revetment shows how little clearance exists between the walls and the guns on their mounts. During gusty conditions or with crosswinds, entering or leaving the revetment is difficult especially when the helicopter's own rotor wash is recirculated by the walls. This recirculation produces turbulent feedback and adverse air currents that make the aircraft somewhat twitchy.

(Above) Specialist 5 (SP-5) Dan Beckerdite and Private First Class (PFC) Dave Ivie, both armorers, smile during the servicing of an M158 seven-tube, 2.75 inch FFAR rocket launcher for a UH-1C. These troops work out of a CONEX shipping container that serves as their workshop and storage facility. A UH-1C gunship the men are working on sits protected in its revetment behind them.

(Below) This Bell UH-1C is one of two in A Troop that is armed with the XM-5 weapons sub-system. This weapons sub-system was comprised of a 40 mm grenade launcher in a nose turret and two M158 rocket launchers. Two M60, 7.62 mm machine guns hung in the aft cabin doors on bungee cords for the gunners.

(Above) The 40 mm grenade launcher's ammunition feet chute feeds into the battery compartment in the nose and aft to the ammunition tanks on the rear cabin floor. This turret was controlled by the copilot, who used a flex sight that lowered from the ceiling above his seat.

(Below) This view is through the pilot's rocket sight. The rocket sight is swung down from the ceiling in an arc and is usually only used when rockets are about to be fired.

(Above) The view through the copilot's Minigun sight. This gun is an "area fire" weapon, and the circle indicates the area where the spray of rounds will hit.

(Below) The view through the copilot's grenade launcher sight. The turret will track where this sight is aimed, both in azimuth and elevation.

(Above) A Hughes OH-6A Cayuse of the Scout Platoon, 7th Squadron, 17th Air Cavalry. This design won the Army's Light Observation Helicopter (LOH) contract and was called the Loach.

(Below) Lt. Dave Huston stands behind a firing Minigun and contends with the noise while he boresights the gun on the range to ensure the gun hits where it aims.

The 17th Air Cavalry Goes Operational

We went operational in November 1967, and one of our first reconnaissance missions for the 4th Infantry Division (4ID) was south to Ban Blech. Here, the Scout Platoon Loaches would recon an area while we orbited overhead in the gunships to cover the scouts. Any trouble the scouts got into was quickly dealt with since we were in position to roll into a dive within approximately 30 seconds and provide covering fire. I always marveled at the sheer "gutsiness" of our scouts. At times, they hovered above a 300 foot triple canopy of jungle while hoping their rotor wash would uncover some worthwhile target or evidence of enemy activity to report back to 4ID. When the troops found some highly vexed and well-armed NVA, their airspeed was usually low, and they were vulnerable to the enemy. The scouts worked in pairs for mutual support.

Only one weapon, a Minigun, is mounted on the left side of the Loach.

(Above) I model the typical combat helicopter pilot fashion: jungle fatigues tucked into my pants, a flight jacket, jungle boots, a web belt complete with a Smith & Wesson .38 caliber revolver, my flight helmet in my bag, and ceramic chest armor nicknamed "chicken plate." The chicken plate is an indispensable fashion accessory.

The Loach's instrument panel is functional and easy-to-read.

30 November 1967. **A CH-47 Chinook (nicknamed "shithook" by the troops) brings a fuel blivet into the airstrip at Ban Blech. This helicopter produces 100 mph worth of rotor wash.**

A CH-47 of the 179th Assault Support Helicopter Company, the "Shrimpboats," hovers over to the POL area at Ban Blech airstrip. The helicopter appears to be a combat veteran with lots of time "in-country."

North to the Dak To Hot Spot

In November 1967, we went north to the airstrip near Dak To village. Some of the war's heaviest fighting occurred in this mountainous region where Vietnam, Laos, and Cambodia come together. The area is defined by steep mountains with sharp karst (limestone terrain characterized by sinks, ravines, and underground streams), deep valleys, and 300 foot tall trees in the jungle, which has a triple canopy where troops need flashlights to make their way through. Artillery fire bases situated atop numerous mountains provided cover and fire support for troops and mechanized cavalry units who conducted sweeps in the valley floors below. The region was pock-marked by bomb craters from F-100s and B-52s.

Dak To is staggeringly beautiful. It also was a crucial area to hold and secure. This region contained the route from the Ho Chi Minh Trail in Laos to the plains of the Central Highlands and the key cities of Kontum and Pleiku. Whoever controlled this region controlled the Central Highlands, and by extension, all of Vietnam.

The 4ID sent us to conduct reconnaissance operations throughout the area. We were ordered to locate, identify, and report. From there, the 4ID decided whether a battle would occur. This assignment was the intended plan. However, the NVA had their own agenda and often took the decision out of the 4ID's hands. Thus, some of the most vicious fights occurred here: the epic battle of Hill 875 fought by the 173rd Airborne Brigade, the battle of Ben Het, the appearance of Russian PT-76 amphibious tanks, and the final rush through this pathway by NVA forces after the American withdrawal in 1975. This region was the theater into which we were thrust to conduct reconnaissance, to find and report, to poke a stick into the hornet's nest, and hopefully, to survive.

30 November 1967. **A Charley-model lands on the rubberized airstrip at Ban Blech. Our unit insignia is painted on the battery compartment cover on the nose–a white stirrup of the cavalry superimposed by the yellow lightning bolt of aviation.**

Dak To airstrip, 20 December 1967. A Sikorsky CH-34 of the 219th Helicopter Company, VNAF, the "Kingbees," awaits a troop lift. The ship is camouflaged in black and green and has an Olive Drab replacement tail pylon.

A CH-34 Kingbee door gunner mans his Browning M1919A6 .30 caliber machine gun.

This CH-34 shows not all landings were entirely successful. The helicopter appears to be a victim of ground resonance.

A Beech U-21 goes down the airstrip in Dak To and carries General Creighton Abrams, the supreme commander in Vietnam, after a conference with local commanders. Abrams' red, four-star placard is evident in the aft cabin window.

Lift Platoon, A Troop Capt. Eddie Mebane finds a shady spot under the tail boom of his UH-1H. The organic infantry, D Troop "Blues," await the call to ride to battle in this ship.

Ban Blech airstrip. An ex-Army de Havilland C-7A Caribou, in USAF markings, carries supplies for the Cessna O-1E Bird Dogs, flown by the Forward Air Controllers (FACs). When the USAF complained the Army had these large, "inappropriate" fixed-wing assets, the Department of Defense made the Army hand them over.

A Cessna O-1E Bird Dog FAC sits in its revetment at the airstrip in Dak To. FACs worked with the F-100s, which came on call from Phu Cat Air Base. The Cessna's revetment makes good use of sandbags and oil drums filled with dirt.

(Above) A USAF Kaman HH-43B Huskie sits at the Dak To airstrip. The rear doors are removed for ventilation and to lighten the ship.

(Below) *22 December 1967.* A UH-1C, belonging to the 119th Assault Helicopter Company "Crocodiles" and based at Camp Holloway in Pleiku, sits on the Dak To airstrip. This ship is armed with the XM-3 weapons sub-system–two 24-tube, 2.75 inch FFAR rocket launchers. Aircraft with this armament were often formed into Aerial Rocket Artillery (ARA) units.

(Above) *Camp Holloway, Pleiku.* A UH-1H, belonging to the lift section of the 170th Assault Helicopter Company "Bikinis," displays its nose art. The Bikinis are assigned to the 52nd Combat Aviation Battalion, "The Flying Dragons." The Playboy character "Little Annie Fannie" is a vivid reminder of home.

(Below) *22 December 1967.* The crew members of the USAF HH-43B await their next mission at Dak To.

A C-130 shows what happens when it gets caught unloading supplies by NVA units. These enemy units were on a mountainside that overlooked the airstrip. Mortars were zeroed in on the airfield area, and the Air Force learned to land only one C-130 at a time to unload while the others orbited overhead and waited.

22 December 1967. Three C-130s were caught on the ground and destroyed by mortars. The remains were bulldozed off the strip into the creek.

(Above) *Dak To sirstrip, 22 December 1967.* A C-130 lands using full flaps, hard braking, and reverse thrust that sends up dust clouds. Watching these planes land was always an event. Sometimes, we bet on whether the planes could stop in time.

(Below) This C-130 had an M151 Mutt on board, which can be seen in the wreckage. A number of the NVA mortar rounds were duds but still accurate enough to punch holes in this C-130's vertical fin.

22 December 1967. A USAF Cessna O-2 FAC refuels at Dak To. Beneath each wing, the aircraft has a rocket launcher that carries seven, 2.75 inch FFARs. These weapons have white phosphorus warheads that make them ideal marking rounds for marking targets for the "fast movers."

22 December 1967. The O-2 instrument panel has a rocket sight on top of the glare shield and to the left of the pilot's flashlight and knee board.

Time To Go...

During this period, we found many NVA units who, unlike the Viet Cong (VC) further south, often stood their ground and preferred to fight. We had a great deal of respect for the NVA. They were well-armed, politically-motivated, generally well-led, and they often fought well. They seemed to have little regard for their enormous losses when they felt their objective was of great political or military value. They were often more ruthless than us, the 17th Air Cavalry "Ruthless Riders."

We continuously made contact with various NVA units in the area around Dak To and often spent days at a time unloading our rockets and Miniguns on targets indicated to us by American ground units who were in contact with them. We expended our ordnance, got relieved on station by two other gunships, then returned to Dak To airstrip to refuel and rearm. After a short break, we returned to the Area of Operations (AO) and relieved that team of gunships so they could replenish. And so it went–shuttle out; shuttle back. Shoot. Refuel. Rearm. Eat. Sleep. Shuttle out. Often, the airstrip was as dangerous as the AO. In the photo below, we just landed, refueled "hot" (with the engine at idle and the rotors turning), then hovered over to the rearming area for a load of rockets and Minigun ammunition. Outside the aircraft, I was screwing rocket warheads onto rocket motors when I heard a sound over the helicopter's noise at flight idle next to me. When we discovered the noise came from NVA mortar rounds exploding in the POL area, which caused a fire and smoke column, we decided half a load of ordnance was better than none. We vacated the area in about 15 seconds. Getting airborne was our primary goal. Putting distance between us and this unwelcome activity was second, and last, when we were able, we found time to fasten our seat belts and shoulder harnesses and close our pilots' doors.

The American response to this inhospitable action was typical. Artillery was called in on the likely sites used by the NVA mortar crews, F-100s brought in ordnance and napalm, M42 "Duster" pieces of armor sprayed the hillside, and we were directed to scout the side of the mountain adjacent to the airstrip to report on the results. Often, little was left to be seen besides huge rents in the jungle. Sometimes, a sizable body count was noted, but occasionally they were still there. And they were angry.

***12 January 1968.* Fuel burns while we waste no time on the ground in this unfriendly neighborhood. The NVA dropped mortar rounds on the POL area moments after we refueled there. We had just vacated that spot and hovered over to the rearming point for more rockets and Minigun ammunition.**

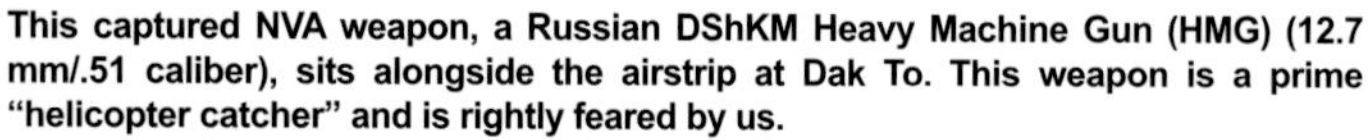

This captured NVA weapon, a Russian DShKM Heavy Machine Gun (HMG) (12.7 mm/.51 caliber), sits alongside the airstrip at Dak To. This weapon is a prime "helicopter catcher" and is rightly feared by us.

American artillery lays a linear sheath of white phosphorus rounds on suspected NVA positions. White phosphorus is not pleasant nor fun to step on. Pieces of it can lie in water for years and then ignite spontaneously when exposed to air.

(Below) This UH-1C gunship, belonging to A Troop, 7th Squadron, 17th Air Cavalry, heads to Camp Enari over the Kontum Valley. This gunship just completed action at Dak To. It carries the XM-21 weapons sub-system. The cabin doors are slid aft for cooling and ventilation, and the door gunners relax for a while. This Charley model is designed as an interim gunship. It hangs from the remarkable Bell 540 "Door Hinge" rotor, which gives it high maneuverability. The helicopter is equipped with a dual hydraulic system for redundancy, and the tail fin is asymmetrical. The vertical fin is concave on the left side, an airfoil which provides an anti-torque moment to the right that unloads the tail rotor at high speed. This design allows more of the available horsepower to be delivered to the main rotor for lift and thrust.

Administrative Flights, Side Trips, and Non-Combat Jaunts

Not all flying involved combat. Sometimes, we needed to visit places, see people, take commanders to consult with other commanders, take downed aircraft their needed parts, pieces, or replacement engines; gather supplies, attend orientations, and share experiences. This type of flying was a welcome break from the daily rigors of combat. However, we usually felt a twinge of guilt that we were "slacking off" while our buddies stayed behind to pull the heavy load of combat. Thus, we reveled in these flights when we could, but we never went out of our way to get them. If one of these flights came our way, we considered the flight something we had to do as merely "one of the hazards of combat." We liked that philosophy. It made us feel less guilty.

Non-combat flights took me to Kontum, An Khe, Qui Nhon, Ban Me Thuot, and other lesser-known cities, towns, and villages in the Central Highlands of Vietnam. I marveled at the stark beauty

The right door gunner has this viewpoint in the aft cabin of a UH-1C gunship. Frank Sheperis, the pilot, wears his APH-5 flight helmet decorated with an elaborate, painted Asian Dragon that shows Frank's artistic ability. The rocket sight is swung up to the left and out of the way, which indicates Frank is not engaged in combat. The padded windshield wiper motor is located above and to the right of Frank's head. The copilot's pantographic gun sight for the Miniguns is in the upper left corner of this photograph. Everyone had a camera, and one is hanging to the left. Some cameras survived the heat, humidity, vibration, and NVA. Some did not.

of this country from the air–the rugged mountains and karst, the various shades of jungle greens, blues, and yellows; the South China Sea's purples, indigos, and aquamarines; and the Central Highlands' reddish-brown plains. I saw Teddy Roosevelt's lavish hunting lodge near Ban Me Thuot, which was a hunter's paradise. I looked down upon pink elephants foraging in the scrub. Their skin was stained pink from bathing in the rivers lined with red clay. I saw Bengal tigers, large peacocks, and water buffalo by the thousands. I watched hundreds of workers tend the emerald-green rice plants in thousands of beautifully-terraced paddies. I flew by ancient statues of Buddha covered in verdigris. The statues sat placidly by the mountain-top temples. I often thought about what a beautiful and scenic country Vietnam was when I took one of these administrative flights. Vietnam would be a first-class tourist Mecca on a level with East Africa if not for the war, and that seemed a pity.

On 19 January 1968, I flew on board a UH-1H sent from Camp Enari, Pleiku, to An Khe for supplies and equipment. An Khe was home to the famous First Air Cavalry Division (Airmobile), and

(Above) *First Air Cavalry Division "Golf Course," 19 January 1968.* The Hueys have three-sided revetments made from 55-gallon oil drums filled with soil and topped with sand bags. The Chinooks in the background have two-sided revetments, which appear more permanent since they are made with steel panels similar to those the USAF uses. An abundance of CONEX shipping containers house parts, tools, and other aircraft supplies. Camp Radcliff sits in the far background.

landing at their huge heliport, "The Golf Course" was a revelation. I was impressed by the sheer number of aircraft in their revetments. An Airmobile division is a large organization, and it often had supplies in abundance. This division did not mind sharing with another Air Cavalry outfit. They made us feel welcome, and these fine people were pleased to show us around.

We got our first up-close look at one of their larger aircraft, the Sikorsky CH-54A "Tarhe." Tarhe is the name of yet another Native American tribe the Army used for naming its aircraft. The troop promptly discarded this naming and call the Tarhe the "Crane."

These massive and stately helicopters were used to deliver bulldozers to mountain tops to build fire bases for artillery. The tracks were delivered separately as a pair to keep the lift weights to a manageable level. The Cranes also moved large pieces of towed artillery to inaccessible locations and recovered downed aircraft. Seeing a Crane flying along with a Huey, Bird Dog, or Mohawk dangling beneath it (a drogue chute trailing to keep the load from spinning) seemed odd. Cranes, or "Skycranes" (Sikorsky's nickname for the helicopter) were responsible for recovering millions of dollars worth of aircraft for repair and rebuild. The Cranes more than paid their way.

Scouts from First Air Cavalry Division use this Bell OH-13 Sioux as a light observation helicopter. The Loach replaced this old workhorse beginning in 1967.

The CH-54 was designed for three pilots to fly it. Two pilots faced forward. The third pilot sat in the aft-facing seat. He was responsible for positioning the Crane over its external load for hook-up and delivery. This pilot had excellent visibility and used a third set of flight controls with limited control authority to accomplish his job. Only senior and very experienced Army Aviators flew these gentle giants.

The CH-54A, aft-facing pilot's station has a third set of flight controls with limited control authority. Though from the back, the view is quite majestic.

19 January 1968. **A Sikorsky CH-54A of the First Air Cavalry Division sits in its revetment at An Khe.**

(Above) The CH-54A instrument panel shows the two vertical rows of engine instruments in the center. Flight instruments are to the right, and caution and warning light capsules are the three rows of rectangles on the left.

(Below) This spindly-looking ship can carry a pod below the fuselage configured for various purposes.

Staging From Kontum Airstrip

The 4th Infantry Division moved us around the area frequently. We flew from one hot spot to another in search of our elusive foe, the NVA. In March 1968, we operated off of Kontum airstrip and supported various units in contact with the NVA out to the west near the airstrip and Plei Mrong fire base. This battlefield became bloody.

This 106 mm recoilless rifle mounted on an M151 is part of the Kontum airfield defenses. The troops who make this emplacement their home are covered with red dirt from the CH-47's rotor wash.

8 March 1968. **A Douglas C-47 (XV-N7B) of Vietnam Air Lines starts its right engine at Kontum airstrip.**

(Above) The instrument panel of the OH-13 has tactical FM radios at the top of the stack, and carburetor heat and mixture levers protrude from the quadrant at the top left. The control sticks are called cyclic pitch levers in a helicopter since they cycle the pitch of the main rotor blades as they rotate to obtain directional movement.

Kontum airstrip, 8 March 1968. **(Below) A Chinook delivers a sling load of ammunition to a unit manning a 106 mm recoilless rifle mounted on an M151 Mutt at Kontum airstrip, The purple smoke marks the drop site, the wind direction, and its velocity.**

(Above) *8 March 1968.* This (presumably) CIA Air America C-123 Provider is likely an ex-USAF B- model. It has Pratt & Whitney R-2800 radial engines but no outboard J85 jet engines that denote the K-model. This mysterious aircraft is on a clandestine mission. The pilots confer by the door while CIDG troops embark via the rear loading ramp.

(Below) *8 March 1968.* A "spook" Fairchild C-123 Provider lands at the Kontum airstrip. Camouflaged in black, light green, and dark green; this aircraft carries no markings of any kind and is used to ferry Civilian Irregular Defense Group (CIDG) troops to various locations where they are needed.

8 March 1968. A Douglas C-47 of the VNAF ends its days quietly in a field alongside Kontum airstrip.

Another Administrative Flight: Coastal City Of Qui Nhon

In March, I took another administrative flight from Pleiku to the east over the mountains to Qui Nhon for essential supplies. Anyone with a sense of history could easily understand the impossible task the French faced as they attempted to regain their former colony of French Indochina in this kind of terrain. As we paralleled Highway 19 and flew eastward towards An Khe and over the Mang Yang Pass, we marked where the French Group Mobile 100 was ambushed by the Viet Minh in 1954. Every twist and turn in the highway, every large and small pass looked ideal for guerilla warfare. Any army tied to the road network was an easy target and likely prey. This mountainous and rugged country made me understand why the United States Army put such emphasis on developing airmobile warfare and why helicopters were vital in this struggle.

While in my helicopter, I thought that militarily, this conflict clearly could be contained using the mobility of the helicopter and the tactics that proved successful on the battlefield. However, I was just a helicopter pilot who had no business ruminating on the politics of why we were in Vietnam or which side was right. Thus, I ended my musing and concentrated on the imminent approach and landing.

The port at Qui Nhon was where I arrived by ship in what seemed a time long ago, and the city looked different from the air. Situated along a coastline of white sand that bordered the South China Sea, the landscape's beauty and the ocean's varied colors were breathtaking. Qui Nhon was a sparkling jewel nestled in a colorful crown. The sharp mountains ran down to the sea and provided me with much to take in visually and admire. The traffic pattern took us out over the harbor on a left base leg before turning final approach to land to the northwest. I found difficulty staying focused on flying and not gazing at the scenery. Every color in the artist's palette was in abundance, right out in front of my aircraft's windscreen. I was destined to spend a fortune on film.

The beach looks inviting as we approach to land on the runway at Qui Nhon. The surf is low, and the sand looks warm. Perhaps the beer is cold. The top of the photograph shows the airfield, and we can make out several C-130s on the ramp.

Some form of amphibious cargo vehicle is recognizable on the beach, perhaps a Lighter, Amphibious Re-Supply Cargo, 15-Ton (LARC-XV). The vehicle shuttles incoming military supplies from the many ships in the harbor to the supply depot.

14 March 1968. A C-130 on final approach to the runway at Qui Nhon sails in over the beach.

14 March 1968. The C-130 taxies to the ramp and past the airfield control tower at Qui Nhon. The rugged beauty of this country, where the mountains march down to the sea, is staggering.

(Below) A CH-47 Chinook, minus its forward rotor system (the rotor head and the three rotor blades), receives major maintenance in its revetment at Qui Nhon airfield. The forward maintenance platforms are lowered around the forward transmission to provide the mechanics with a work platform. In the distance, several UH-1s bask in the sun on the parking ramp while a USAF O-1E Bird Dog glides in for a landing. The mountaintop sprouts radar and other high-powered communication antennae.

An Air America C-46 soldiers on for the CIA. It looks resplendent in its polished, natural metal finish. This plane is lithe and lively, and its engines make a sweet sound. The C-46 appears well-taken care of as it waltzes by. We salute its beauty.

14 March 1968. A Pilatus Turbo Porter of Air America crosses the runway threshold. This Swiss-made, turbine-powered airplane has near-helicopter performance capabilities such as the ability to hover in a strong wind.

(Above) Normally, the Chinook's cockpit is spacious next to the Huey's, but this cockpit is crowded with gear such as a Decca navigation set mounted on the glare shield.

(Below) *Qui Nhon, 14 March 1968.* A UH-1C of the 174th Assault Helicopter Company "Sharks" shows its battle wounds as it undergoes repair. The helicopter has flown through the blast of its own rockets and is perforated throughout. This unit had permission from the original "Flying Tigers" to paint the shark mouth marking on their Hueys.

(Above) The Mohawk's cockpit is complex.

(Above) Chinooks are generally armed with an M60, 7.62 mm machine gun in the left, forward window. The gun provides suppressive fire during operations in forward areas.

(Below) A Grumman OV-1 Mohawk gets its daily inspection.

25

War Heats Up At Ban Me Thuot

In March 1968, the North Vietnamese Army increased their activity in our area, and we often found ourselves engaged with small NVA units west of Ban Me Thuot. The Ho Chi Minh Trail was a two-lane road that ran south through Laos and Cambodia and had many branches stemming east to various points in Vietnam. We found many NVA heading toward us on these routes and eager to fight. We became sober and serious during this period as our casualties mounted. My pilot's logbook excerpts paint a picture of the combat thus far:

- "Major Charlie had his thumb shot off during this fight."
- "Scout pilot Lt. Sierra shot in leg; made it back okay."
- "Pilot Romeo on night gun run had rocket launcher explode, possibly from a hit. Shot down at Kontum."
- "Pilots Papa and Romeo shot down and wounded."
- "Pilot Romeo's C-model crashed outside the perimeter wire."
- "Large battle near Cambodian border, two U.S. companies surrounded, artillery falling through our orbit, swept NVA snipers out of trees with Miniguns."
- "Lt. Sierra's Loach shot down, his observer was killed."
- "Flew Troop Commander to cover crash of UH-1C, crew chief Sierra killed. Aircraft lifted out by Chinook."
- "Took eight rounds through ship, door gunner Echo shot in chest. Aircraft #66649 took 6 rounds".
- "Captain Bravo had ship shot up near Polei Kleng."
- "Aircraft #66727 shot down with Lt. Hotel at controls. Pilot Sierra and crew chief Delta with broken backs. We destroyed the aircraft with rockets."
- "Lt. Papa's C-model crashed."
- "Delta Papa's Loach downed, everyone okay."
- "Pilot Tango's C-model took hits, shot down, Tango has two broken legs. Medevac'd out."

Ban Me Thuot, 24 March 1968. **The Green Hornets' UH-1F refuels "hot." The Green Hornet insignia on the tail boom indicates the USAF 20th Special Operations Squadron (SOS). This model has a baggage bay on the right side of the tail boom. The designation was changed to UH-1P on June 1969.**

A USAF UH-1F from the 20th SOS "Green Hornets" refuels at Ban Me Thuot airfield with two others. The side exhaust marks the installation of the General Electric T58 engine that is also used in the CH-3E.

A UH-1C with old style XM157 rocket launchers and no guns lands at Ban Me Thuot for fuel. The airfield control tower in the left distance carries radar, which is unusual for remote strips such as this one.

24 March 1968. **An Air America Beech Model 18 N137L sits on the ramp at Ban Me Thuot airfield. The airplane is spotless with a polished natural metal finish and sparkles in the morning sun.**

The field holds the remains of a UH-1C that was shot down over the highway between Pleiku and Kontum. The Huey's magnesium and aluminum structure burned readily. We saw this fact all too often.

As our combat and non-combat losses mounted, we engaged in some sober reflection. At no time did we feel we were losing the war or that our tactics were poor. All the statistics provided to us by the ground units we supported showed just the opposite. The statistics proved to us, at least in military terms, that we were decimating the NVA units who hurled themselves against us. The body counts, the weapons captured, and the formations we shattered all showed that the aircraft we flew, the tactics we employed, and the artillery and tactical air assets we used when we needed something bigger were the proper solutions to this conflict.

What gave us pause for thought was our rate of attrition over just a few months of combat. This attrition rate was a measure of the NVA's tenacity. The excellent weapons readily supplied to them by China and the USSR also helped them fight as well as they did. We were fighting against a formidable and well-equipped regular army in the Central Highlands, not the hit-and-run guerilla warfare tactics employed by the Viet Cong further south. Our losses demonstrated this fact.

Over time, we were filled with a growing awareness that the odds did not favor any of us completing our required one-year tour of duty in Vietnam, especially if the rate of attrition continued. The fact dawned on us that many of our group, if not most, eventually would be killed. At 19, 20, or even 21 years of age, our youth made us feel invulnerable and invincible. We knew people would get killed, but "the other guy" would get killed, not us. We were going to live forever.

However, we now saw the possibility, perhaps probability, that we would die. We saw this fact quite clearly.

We struggled with that concept for some time. The period for this struggle was very personal. Some people took months to work their way through the struggle. Others only took a few weeks. After a great deal of ruminating and introspection, many of my fellow air crew members gradually accepted the concept of their own demise. They accepted the fact that they would not live through Vietnam, that they would eventually get killed. However, until that time came, they had missions to fly, friends to cover, and buddies to support.

Basically, we had a job to do, a duty to perform. While no patriotic flag-waving occurred (at least not among us front-line troops who were actually fighting), we operated as a cohesive unit because of camaraderie, because we knew the other guy. Whether in a cockpit, behind a door gun, or on the ground, we knew the other guy was counting on us to do our job. Thus, we accepted the eventuality of our own death. Once we accepted this fact, something remarkable happened.

We no longer carried the heavy burden of fear, of concern, of emotion. Without this burden, we were lifted to a higher performance level. We gained sharper vision, improved hearing, and enhanced abilities to grasp tactical situations and picture them in our minds. We received the gift of total clarity and found we operated on a higher plane. In short, we became better pilots.

This mental state did not mean we were free from being afraid at times, nor did it imply we were foolhardy or wanted to die. We simply left our emotions and our "selves" on the ground. We flew like we were one with the aircraft. Someone once explained to me that psychologically, this attitude was a "leaving of the self," a type of chrysalis. We became something better. We flew more intuitively since we were not dogged by the fear of dying. Perhaps this chrysalis is why we survived.

(Above) *24 March 1968.* An NVA AK-47 assault rifle made this hole in the aircraft floor beneath my seat.

(Below) *24 March 1968.* The round impacted the bottom of my pilot's seat. The seat's bottom consists of a ceramic armor (boron carbide), which stopped the round. This round was one of eight we counted in my aircraft.

(Above) This view shows the left side of the vertical fin of the aircraft where a large-caliber round made a hole in the tail rotor drive shaft between the 42 degree gearbox on the left and the 90 degree gearbox up higher. The drive shaft twisted a few degrees but never severed. Had it severed, I would have lost tail rotor control, which is a first-class emergency in any helicopter pilot's book.

(Below) Another AK-47 round came up through the aircraft floor and through my flight helmet bag where my Army-issued flashlight stopped it. The bullet is still on the flashlight. If not for the flashlight, the round would have gone through the lens of my camera, a very nice Minolta. I still shudder at the thought of that happening.

DEPARTMENT OF THE ARMY
HEADQUARTERS 17TH COMBAT AVIATION GROUP
APO San Francisco 96240

GENERAL ORDERS
NUMBER 66

23 August 1968

AWARD OF THE PURPLE HEART

1. TC 320. The following AWARDS are announced.
Awd: As indic
Date action: As indic in SNL
Theater: Republic of Vietnam
Reason: For wounds received in connection with military operations against a hostile force
Auth: By direction of the President under the provisions of AR 672-5-1

RAYL, CHARLES R. OF104242 (SSAN ██████) CPT AR A Trp 7/17th Air Cav APO 96262; 9 Mar 68
STEINBRUNN, ROBERT N. W3155719 (SSAN ██████) CW2 AVN 189th Avn Co APO 96318; 24 Mar 68
WINTERRATH, JOSEPH H. W3157239 (SSAN ██████) CW2 AVN 170th Avn Co APO 96318; 27 Feb 68
MATHEWS, STANLEY E. III W3157846 (SSAN ██████) WO1 AVN 170th Avn Co APO 96318; 14 Jan 68
MCDONOUGH, JOSEPH V JR. W3159030 (SSAN ██████) WO1 AVN 189th Avn Co APO 96318; 26 Mar 68
RAMSEY, JAMES D. RA16741044 (SSAN ██████) SGT E5 189th Avn Co APO 96318; 2 Feb 68
SYLVESTER, HARVEY JR. RA55985192 (SSAN ██████) SP4 E4 225th Avn Co APO 96316; 4 Aug 68
Awd: Purple Heart

KISER, JAMES D. RA11550440 (SSAN ██████) SP4 E4 225th Avn Co APO 96316; 4 Aug 68
Awd: Purple Heart (First Oak Leaf Cluster)

FOR THE COMMANDER:

OFFICIAL:

JOSEPH C. LE FLORE
1LT, AGC
Asst Adjutant

JERALD M GOOCH
1LT, AGC
Adjutant

DISTRIBUTION:
5-Ea indiv conc; 5-225th Avn Co
5-A Trp 7/17th ACS; 5-189th Avn Co
5-170th Avn Co; 5-223d Avn Bn
5-HHT 7/17th ACS; 5-52d Avn Bn
5-1st Avn Bde, ATTN: AVBA-A
5-USARV, ATTN: AVHAG-PF
1-Ea indiv 201 File
1-Rec Set; 1-Ref Set

SPECIAL DISTRIBUTION:
5-TAGO, ATTN: AGPF-F
3-TAGO, ATTN: AGPE-F
3-CINCUSARPAC, ATTN: AG-DP
3-CINCUSARPAC, ATTN: AROP-MA
1-Dir, OPD, ATTN: OPO-AR
1-Dir, OPD, ATTN: OPO-WO

(Top Left) These official orders award the Purple Heart to the author, who says, "On 24 March 1968, I flew in a UH-1C gunship with Alpha Troop, 7th Squadron, 17th Cavalry. We were conducting reconnaissance missions west of Ban Me Thuot on behalf of the 4th Infantry Division. As our four gunships swept over some sparsely forested scrubland at approximately 500 feet of altitude, our cockpit "exploded" in a torrent of small fire, bullets, broken glass, and shards of plexiglass from the windshield and overhead windows. We had overflown an NVA battalion without seeing them in their camouflaged positions. They held their fire until we had almost flown past them. They knew we could not shoot well to our rear. Our flight of two gunships circled back to where the fire originated, and we expended most of our rockets and Minigun ammunition on the area. These events happened very quickly. My ship was the only one hit. Not knowing how badly our aircraft was damaged, our flight of two gunships departed the area. We left the other flight of two aircraft on station and flew back to Ban Me Thuot. Once there, we shut down and inspected the aircraft for combat damage. Our maintenance personnel grounded the helicopter until the tail rotor drive was replaced; then they declared it capable of being ferried by a maintenance team back north to Camp Enari (our base camp) for permanent repairs. During the NVA fire, I was grazed across my ankle by an AK-47 bullet. Additionally, both my knee caps got grazed by another AK-47 bullet, which scored them. I did not realize I was injured at the time it happened. I was too busy. Being surprised by the NVA in this manner was not the most glamorous way to win a Purple Heart."

(Middle) A VNAF O-1E Bird Dog lays forlornly by the Ban Me Thuot runway. The plane is a victim of a bad landing by a wounded pilot. These planes are used as artillery spotters and FAC aircraft. They sport one long FM radio antenna above and two 2.75 inch, FFAR rocket tubes beneath each wing. The fuselage is Olive Drab. The wing's upper surface is light gray to make the airplane more conspicuous from above.

(Bottom) ***Ban Me Thuot, 24 March 1968.*** **A Sikorsky CH-54A lifts up to carry the Bird Dog away to a rear echelon repair facility. Normally, these heavy-lift assets were not used on such light loads.**

Flight of a Lifetime

After months of eating Army chow in our mess tent, some of us eventually discovered the wonders of the USAF Officers' Open Mess at Pleiku Airbase, a short distance north of Camp Enari. The culinary delights at this dining facility were a sharp contrast to what we were used to, and the regular tables with chairs and silverware seemed too exquisite to imagine. During one of these forays into Air Force civilization, I met Major Gerould A. Young of the 6th Air Commando Squadron. He noticed me when I sat down at the table across from him. When he saw I and the others with me were from the Army and were pilots, he asked what type of aircraft we flew. When he heard we flew UH-1C Huey gunships, his eyes lit up. In an animated voice, he described how he took an orientation ride in one. He was allowed to fire the Miniguns at low level, an exciting proposition anytime, and he waxed eloquently on the thrills and adventures he was certain we all were having. Based on his level of enthusiasm, I thought he was an administrative or cargo pilot. I asked what type of aircraft he flew.

"Oh, you know, one of those old A-1s," he said and dismissively waved his hand.

My mouth hung open.

"A Douglas Skyraider?" I tried to confirm.

"Yes, one of those," he added matter-of-factly.

I was dumbfounded. Of all the toys available to boys, the A-1 must surely rank close to the top of the list. This chance meeting with Major Young led me to the opportunity to fly in one.

(Above) ***Pleiku Airbase, 20 April 1968.*** **This sign identifies the 6th Air Commando Squadron (ACS).**

(Below) ***20 April 1968.*** **A Douglas A-1H runs up its engine prior to a mission. The exhaust noise of the Wright R-3350 is ear-splitting. The 6th ACS tail code is ET. This aircraft has yet to be armed.**

(Above) An armed A-1H of the 6th ACS sits in its steel revetment with six MK-82, 500-pound bombs and two MK-117, 750-pound bombs. A 300-gallon centerline drop tank and four 20 mm cannon in the wings complete the package. USAF Major "Gerry" A. Young chats with my buddy and fellow Army pilot, Michael E. Smith.

(Below) *24 April 1968.* A closer look at '059's ordnance load. These airplanes have that nice "lived in" look.

(Above) The single-seat A-1H's instrument panel has that 1950s look. The gauges are, from the top left, radar (or radio) altimeter gauge. Middle row: airspeed indicator, standby attitude indicator (or artificial horizon), vertical velocity (or rate of climb) indicator, main attitude indicator, drop tank fuel gauge. Bottom row: altimeter, Radio Magnetic Indicator (RMI), slip-skid (turn and bank) indicator, Tactical Air Navigation (TACAN) indicator, Distance Measuring Equipment (DME) readout, an engine gauge that shows cylinder head temperature, engine oil temperature, and engine oil pressure. At the very bottom is the armament control panel, which has a yellow knob that selects which wing stations drop what ordnance.

(Below) The gun sight reflector glass has a curved inclinometer, also called a slip-skid indicator, to show when the ship is in perfect trim. This information is a necessity with aircraft, whether helicopters or airplanes, firing rockets. The sight is padded for the pilot's face protection. To the left, a setting knob is in place. This knob adjusts the sight to the ballistics of the specific ordnance that the aircraft is expending at the moment. An accelerometer is housed in front of the sight. It is the typical "G"-meter that is necessary when carrying heavy ordnance loads in high performance aircraft.

I first had to secure permission from the Commanding Officer (CO) of A Troop. I explained to him what I proposed to do and presented him with a "hold harmless" form that required his signature. This form originated from the 7th Air Force (the parent organization of the 6th ACS), and it basically said if I augured in during the air strike, the USAF was not at fault. My CO arched an eyebrow and asked me why I wanted to ride with the Air Force. I discarded phrases such as "flight of a lifetime" and "thrills, chills, and spills in a Skyraider." Instead, I emphasized the importance of being "oriented" by the Air Force and having this "familiarization" conducted by them since we occasionally coordinated our missions with tactical air (TACAIR) and had worked with A-1s previously.

"Oh," he said, "You can go. This seems like it would be the flight of a lifetime."

I showed up at the 6th ACS operations building on the appointed day and bid Gerry Young hello. He introduced me to his wing man, Lt. Colonel Wallace A. "Jack" Ford, who was actually the team leader but who was conducting a lead pilot checkout on Gerry. Therefore, he would fly wing that day. Both men thought a Huey gunship pilot wanting to fly in an old A-1 was odd, but since I was in the *Army*, they overlooked my idiosyncratic behavior. Fair enough, I thought. It was an inexpensive price to pay.

Gerry conducted a thorough briefing using a mission book as a guide, and we went through a litany of frequencies, call signs, ordnance on board, emergency procedures, and rescue assets. This instruction took over an hour and seemed a broad departure from the "you get mortared; you get airborne" briefing I was used to.

After the briefing, we went to the flight equipment room where we gathered and donned a parachute harness, a survival vest, a personal weapon, and a flight helmet. We then went to the flight line to meet the crew chief of the aircraft we would fly, an A-1G (serial 32612). Gerry received a briefing from his crew chief on the status of the airplane, the ordnance load he would carry, and any outstanding discrepancies. Gerry signed for the aircraft and then conducted a walk-around, pre-flight inspection. When satisfied, he climbed up on an oily wing, bid me do the same, and we buckled in.

The right side console of the A-1H has circuit breakers in the lower left, the gyro compass control panel, various switches for pitot heat, engine oil dilution, and the electrical generator. The rectangular lever is used to spread and fold the wings hydraulically, and aft are various radio control panels.

The A-1 has no ejection seat, which is unusual for a tactical fighter-bomber. The A-1 design dates back to the late 1940s when ejection seats were still under development. Installation of the Yankee Extraction System rather than a "hot" seat was deemed more efficacious when decisions were made to provide the plane with a modern egress system. This system is comprised of a rocket mounted on the cockpit bulkhead behind the pilot. The rocket is attached to the pilot's parachute harness. When the pilot decides the A-1 is no longer "home," he initiates the extraction sequence. First, the canopy section over the pilot is blown off. (In the two-seater we flew, the plane had two sections, one over each pilot. These sections were normally opened and closed electrically by a switch.) Once the canopy section blew, the rocket fired vertically upwards and dragged the pilot out behind it. Thereafter, the rocket burned out and separated from the parachute harness. Normal parachute deployment then occurred. I hoped no ejections would be necessary during my flight.

Firing up the Wright R-3350 engine was an art. Certain preliminary checks were made, then Gerry saluted his crew chief and waved the chocks away. We taxied out to a run-up area where final engine checks were made. Satisfied with these checks, Gerry taxied to an arming area by the runway where the "Remove Before Flight" armament safety pins and flags were pulled. The armorers gave us

This A-1E is fitted with AN-M1A4 Fragmentation Clusters. These clusters arrive on the munitions trailer in units of six bombs per cluster, six clusters per suspension rack, for a total of 36 fragmentation bombs per rack. These bombs disperse over a wide area and are anti-personnel bombs.

(Above) The canopy bow has some minor paint chipping on this single-seat A-1H. The armor glass plate shows up well under the windscreen while the gun sight, with its reflector glass, dominates the pilot's view. In the lower left corner, just inside the glare shield, sits a gray dome ashtray. The steel revetments house a variety of ex-United States Navy, A-1 single and multi-seat versions of the venerable Skyraider, which is painted in USAF Southeast Asia (SEA) camouflage and markings.

(Below) A-1E '038 carries an imposing load of these fragmentation clusters. Despite the highly visible "Remove Before Flight" flags that are attached to safety pins, some of the flags have made it airborne for various reasons.

(Above) *Pleiku Airbase.* USAF Major Gerould A. Young stands on top of an oily airplane wing, hangs his flight helmet on a step, and prepares to climb aboard his A-1G.

(Below) *20 April 1968.* The cockpit of the two-seat A-1G shows the rocket for the Yankee Extraction System, just behind my seat, that waits to carry me safely aloft. I hope I do not have to use this system.

(Above) The instrument panel of the two-seat A-1G is similar to the single-seat A-1H except for the extra room available on the right side for a stack of radio gear. I touch nothing. I sit quietly. I make a determined effort to avoid the Yankee Extraction System lanyard in the seat.

(Below) As Gerry starts the engine, his crew chief monitors the process from outside and watches for fuel or oil leaks. The trash can is for anything that might cause Foreign Object Damage (FOD) to the airplane. The 20 mm cannons and two of the 500-pound bombs are evident. Their arming fuses have propellers locked with safety wire that will pull away when the bombs are dropped. I am told mentioning if I see any rotating propellers while the bombs are still attached is okay to do. Someone with oily boots has walked on the oily wing.

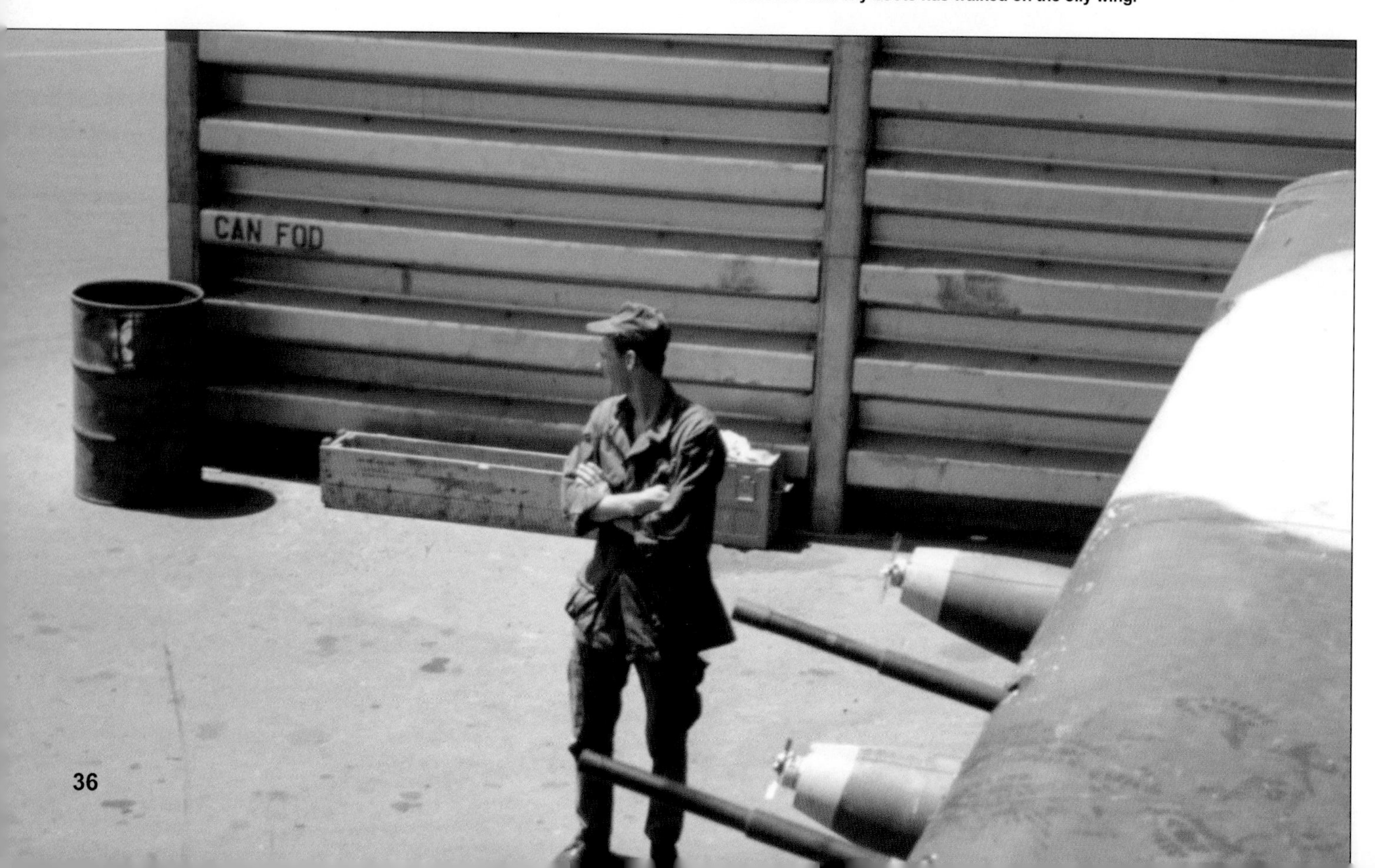

(Above) Lt. Col. Jack Ford runs up his A-1H with "Super Spad One" painted on the cowling. My canopy section is still open, and I think Jack is making a lot of noise. He will lower his seat electrically when he has to close his canopy. I am convinced the many hand holds on the fuselage are there to keep the pilot from sliding off the oily wing.

(Below) An A-1G completes its landing roll as we sit in the arming area prior to takeoff. The aft cabin under the blue canopy sections has room for another six passengers.

After takeoff and aircraft cleanup, Jack flies right echelon so we can look over each other's planes for any abnormalities that might scrub the mission. The Wright R-3350 engine applies 2,700 horses to that huge Aeroproducts propeller, which is very close to my wing tip.

a thumbs-up, and both aircraft taxied into position in the runway. Gerry and Jack coordinated every step of this process with a simple "Spad three, Spad four" series of acknowledgments on the radio using their call signs.

Takeoff clearance from Pleiku Tower came immediately. Then, we were ready to go. Even with a full armament load and the amount of fuel we carried, I thought the acceleration was brisk. Gerry was too busy to explain things to me, but I noticed he did not use full throttle until the airspeed built and the rudder became more effective. He used the remainder of the throttle, and we were up and away. With safe altitude, airspeed, and post-takeoff checks complete, he said Jack would be formating in left and right echelon to allow both pilots to look over each other's aircraft for abnormalities, which might cancel the mission.

We looked each other over, and since all seemed okay, we climbed out to the east toward Qui Nhon. Our FAC called and had targets for us. He had watched some buildings in a rural area for days and was certain NVA activity was occurring there. We made seven separate dives on this target to drop our bombs and expended most of our 20 mm ammunition. We got several large, secondary explosions from the buildings, and the FAC exulted in his success. The buildings contained stored explosives and weapons, rice, and clothing. Our mission presented the NVA with a major set-back.

I cringed during the dives. They were so steep, I had to brace my feet against the forward bulkhead. Gerry pulled 7 "Gs" on each recovery, and my vision grew dark. It narrowed my vision down to a tube, which focused on the accelerometer that pointed to "7." My 3 ½-pound APH-5 flight helmet felt like it weighed 25 pounds. I tried to look over to see if Gerry was still conscious, but I could not move my head. I could not reach the ejection lanyard if Gerry was blacked-out. I realized why these conditions were called "the hazards of combat."

After the strike and during the return to base (RTB), Gerry made several aileron rolls to see if they phased out a helicopter pilot. He was pleased that they did.

We called Pleiku Approach Control and asked for a practice Ground Controlled Approach (GCA), which is an instrument let-down performed by the pilot based on instructions from a specialist in a radar van on the ground. We were vectored straight in to the revetment area well off the runway center line. My eyes got wider as we headed for the parked airplanes, of which many were armed and fueled. Gerry grinned, broke off the approach, sidestepped to the runway, landed, and then laughed. Though I was not certain that the situation was funny, I laughed too. As we taxied in, we opened our canopies for ventilation. The cockpit was air-conditioned the entire mission, but we were soaked with sweat. G-forces tended to wring the sweat out of us even if we felt cool. Taxiing in with the propeller wash blowing in our faces felt especially refreshing.

A momentary gust of wind caused me to drop my camera's lens cover on the cockpit floor. I looked down to a maze of plumbing, switches, and multi-colored knobs and handles and decided to leave the lens cover there. One of these items could be the lanyard for the Yankee Extraction System. After shutdown, I confessed to the crew chief, and he agreed to retrieve my lens cover. As I left the area, I thought I heard him muttering, "*Army!*"

Rest In Peace, Jack

When I returned to Alpha Troop, 7th Squadron, 17th Air Cavalry, I checked in with my CO to report my safe return. He noted my sweat-stained jungle fatigues, crumpled flight jacket, and blood-shot eyes.

"How did your 'orientation' and 'familiarization' go?" he asked. He gave a hint of a smile.

I told him the flight was an "informative" and "invaluable" experience. I gave him a thumbs-up, thanked him for giving permission for me to go, and rendered a snappy salute.

He laughed and said, "From the looks of you, it must have been the flight of a lifetime."

This story has a sad ending. Several weeks after my flight, Jack was killed in action. One source gave the date as 24 May 1968, exactly one month after my flight. Another source states 6 June 1968 as the date. The exact circumstances of Jack's death were equally uncertain. I was told Jack was on another air strike and lost one outboard wing panel. This loss might have been caused by a NVA heavy-caliber, anti-aircraft shell that struck the wing fold hinge. The wing panel might have been lost due to a 20 mm wing cannon malfunction, which fed a live round into the chamber against one that was already there. The end result was the same–without the outboard wing section, Jack's A-1 tumbled.

When he punched out, the aircraft was inverted. The Yankee Extraction System dragged him down through the trees below. I am not sure of all the facts and was told the circumstances third-hand, but I don't think that really matters. What does matter is another outstanding pilot is no longer with us, and I know Jack is missed by many. That many includes me.

Thanks for the flight, Jack. You were great. Sorry about my being so.......*Army!*

This story illustrates, I think, how differing perspectives color the way we see the world. During the flight, Gerry let go of the control stick to make some notes. Since I trained on and flew a Huey, I instinctively grabbed the control stick because a Huey has no stability other than that provided by the pilot. Letting go of the stick is simply never done in a helicopter without an autopilot or flight director. Otherwise, a Huey would fall over. I did not realize the A-1 would drone on quite happily unattended because airplanes were inherently stable. I thought how safe A-1 flying was compared to flying helicopter gunships.

I have since changed my mind.

At 15,000 feet, the tropical atmosphere seems worlds away from the helicopter pilot's domain of tree tops and muddy landing zones. The aileron trim tab seems to be a replacement item that still has its zinc chromate finish.

Vung Tau: In-Country Rest and Relaxation

Troops in Vietnam were given one in-country Rest and Relaxation (R & R) trip. This trip was usually taken at Vung Tau on the coast, southeast of Saigon, and was three days in length. A beautiful resort town, Vung Tau was named Cap Saint Jacques by the French, and they shared its delightful beaches with the Viet Minh, much as we did with the NVA and Viet Cong. A tacit understanding seemed to exist about the war not touching this pearl on the South China Sea, at least not until the time was right.

I boarded a USAF C-7A Caribou from Hensel Field at Camp Enari to Tan Son Nhut Airbase in Saigon, where I was scheduled to switch to a helicopter for the 125 kilometer flight to Vung Tau. After landing at the sprawling airbase, we were told that both Tan Son Nhut and Saigon were under attack by VC. Thus, the helicopter flight was cancelled. We were advised to find a ride to a nearby hotel and to await developments. This event illustrated one of the ironies and contradictions of the conflict in Vietnam. A war was going on. All flights in and out of the airport were cancelled due to fighting on the perimeter, but we were told to find a hotel, have a cool beer, and wait out the fighting. We obeyed orders.

Some CBS TV crews and correspondents offered us a ride in their vehicle to a nearby hotel, and we gratefully accepted. On the way, we saw large columns of smoke from VNAF Skyraiders dropping their ordnance on VC units in the Cholon (Chinese) section of Saigon, just three city blocks from where we stood. Large 122 mm rockets fired by the VC impacted inside the airport, created large craters, and sprayed various aircraft with chunks of asphalt and fragments. We thought these events were too close for vacationers. Thus, we decided to immediately vacation elsewhere.

We stayed in the hotel for two days and had a delightful time sipping beer and watching the battles from the roof. We thought we would have to pack up soon and head for home since our three days were just about over. After much effort, I was able to call my CO on a military line and advise him of the tactical situation. Bless his heart. He said the time in the hotel did not count. My CO told me to head for Vung Tau when able and to stay for the full three days. Compassion truly did exist in the military. I saw this compassion time and time again.

***6 May 1968.* Smoke rises from the Cholon section of Saigon on the edge of Tan Son Nhut airport. VC 122 mm rockets and VNAF A-1s bombing VC launch sites caused the smoke. A number of rockets impacted in this area, and we decided retiring to the library for brandy and cigars was a good idea. To the left, a UH-1 sits in its sandbagged revetment hoping not to become a casualty. Another UH-1 sits in the center of the photo facing the other way. About 50 meters to the right of the UH-1 sits the fuel truck, about to be hit. It was time to leave.**

We were able to link up with our helicopter transportation in due time, and the one hour and fifteen minute flight out to Vung Tau in a UH-1H as a passenger was enjoyable. I had no responsibilities other than to sit by the open cargo door, enjoy the scenery, and take photographs. It was wonderful.

We spent the three days on the beach. We toured the lovely town, enjoyed the ocean vistas, and ate real meals cooked in a real kitchen. We found time to wander back out to the airfield where we saw our first AH-1G Huey Cobras, which were only a rumor up until that point. These helicopters looked lean and lethal and light years ahead of our C-model Huey gunships. We were envious and schemed how to effect a transfer to a unit that flew these helicopters.

Later, I learned these helicopters were not so desirable, at least not the initial models, without air-conditioning. The Huey Cobras had blue-tinted canopies to reflect some of the sun's heat, but later, we watched in amazement at refueling sites as the Cobras landed. The pilots climbed out of their cockpits, collapsed on the ground, and begged for water. I also wondered what tactics they had to evolve to compensate for not having the two door gunners we enjoyed in our Hueys. Both gunners we had could fire aft and down, which covered our break off a target. The pilots in the Huey Cobras seemed vulnerable in this regard. Time would tell.

9 May 1968. An AH-1G Huey Cobras sits on its pad.

A CH-47 sits in its hangar at Tan Son Nhut airport. This aircraft suffered numerous punctures from a 122 mm rocket, fired by VC, that impacted on the ramp and sprayed fragments and chunks of asphalt.

(Above) _6 May 1968._ An Army of the Republic of South Vietnam (ARVN) M24 Chaffee light tank sits in a sandbagged emplacement. On the way to the hotel, we passed through Tan Son Nhut security where we encountered the tank.

(Below) _8 May 1968._ Opening the cargo door of a UH-1H Huey reveals Vung Tau's beautiful view. The harbor is filled with ships, craft, and docking platforms. The airfield is in the middle right of this photograph. We entered a left downwind leg in the traffic pattern. The South China Sea sparkled in the distance, and the beaches beckoned. We could hardly wait.

(Above) *9 May 1968.* A Bell AH-1G Huey Cobra basks in the Vung Tau sun. The troops simply called it a "Cobra," or more commonly, a "Snake." This helicopter is armed with four M200, 2.75 inch FFAR rocket launchers that hold 19 rockets each. This configuration is called the "heavy hog."

(Below) A Lycoming T53-L-703 turboshaft engine with 1,800 shaft horsepower (shp) powers the Cobra.

(Above) The M28 turret carries a single General Electric GAU-2B/A 7.62 mm Minigun. The copilot/gunner sits up front and controls the turret. The pilot sits in back and normally fires the rockets.

(Below) The copilot/gunner enters the front cockpit from here. The blue-tinted canopy reflects the sun.

(Above) The gunner has a rudimentary instrument panel with basic flight, navigation, and engine controls. His audio panel is on the upper left with a communication radio below the panel. He has a cyclic control stick on the right side panel for directional control and a stub collective lever on the left, which is the "up and down" lever. The gunner's primary job concerns the flexible gun sight, which controls the front turret. The weapons in the turret evolved with the Cobra.

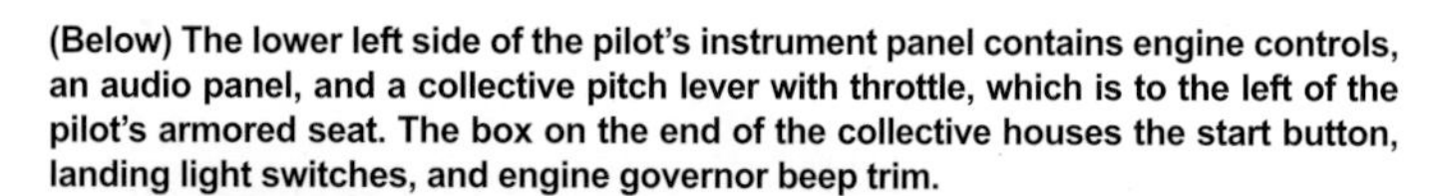

(Above) Bell's semi-rigid "door hinge" rotor system gives the Cobra good maneuverability and the capacity for making a great deal of noise. The main rotor mast connects to the transmission.

(Below) The lower left side of the pilot's instrument panel contains engine controls, an audio panel, and a collective pitch lever with throttle, which is to the left of the pilot's armored seat. The box on the end of the collective houses the start button, landing light switches, and engine governor beep trim.

The pilot's rocket sight sits on top of his instrument panel, and his view is over the top of the gunner, who sits lower in the aircraft. A slip-skid trim indicator is part of any rocket sight.

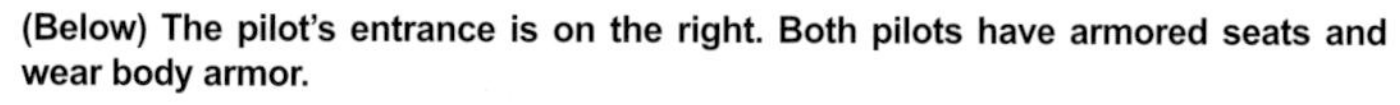

(Above) The pilot's instrument panel has flight and navigation instruments on the top two rows, while engine and transmission instruments are the smaller ones to the lower left.

(Below) The pilot's entrance is on the right. Both pilots have armored seats and wear body armor.

The 52nd CAB memorial wall holds the names of those who have "gone west."

Transfer to The "Ghostriders"

With the influx of new aviation units in Vietnam, some units had a lack of experienced pilots while other units were top-heavy with old hands. Thus, an "infusion" program was implemented. In this program, pilots transferred to other units to spread this experience around. A number of us received notification that we were "it," and we were allowed to indicate our preference for which unit we wanted. Allowing us to indicate a preference was unusual for the Army.

Camp Holloway was home to the 52nd Combat Aviation Battalion (CAB) "Flying Dragons." The camp was located to the north of Camp Enari, about four "klicks" (kilometers), just on the east side of Pleiku. The CAB was the parent organization to a number of smaller aviation units, and one of these units was the 189th Assault Helicopter Company. I hitched a ride to interview with their commanding officer, Major William W. Fraker, to see if he would accept me into his unit. Major Fraker was personable and pleasant. He welcomed me and said the proper paperwork would be processed expeditiously. I hauled my gear to Camp Holloway to be a lift pilot on 15 May 1968, and moved into the Scarlet Platoon hooch.

The flying at Camp Holloway was vastly different from the flying I previously knew. I first had to transition into the Bell UH-1H long-cabin Huey, which was much different from a C-model gunship. I then had to fly along as a copilot for several missions so I could see how the 189th Assault Helicopter Company operated. One week later, after an Aircraft Commander flight checkride, I became Ghostrider 22 and was released to fly on my own with a copilot and crew. Both the crew members were door gunners who manned the M60 machine guns. One of the door gunners was the aircraft's crew chief or its primary mechanic. I always felt reassured to know the aviation technician who tinkered with my aircraft had to fly in it too.

Flying with the "Ghostriders" was always interesting, always varied, perhaps more demanding, and I could see the level of risk was at least equal to flying gunships if not vastly greater. We received our mission sheets in the morning from the Operations Office (mission orders came down from Battalion), and we were gone all day where we conducted anywhere from one to ten separate missions. One mission might consist of flying a single-aircraft to Point "A" to pick up an ARVN artillery commander and his staff, flying them to ARVN artillery unit "B" for conferences and unit "C" for inspection, and flying them back to "A." Another mission might consist of joining two or three other 189th H-models and flying to Kontum or Dak To airfield to load up supplies, ammunition, mail, replacement troops, and hot meal cans. Once we loaded up, we then flew these supplies to various mountaintop fire bases in the area. Yet another mission might consist of locating a mechanized cavalry unit to evacuate their sick and wounded.

Often, no landing zones existed when we found these troops out in the bush. Sometimes the troops used their M113 ACAV "tracks" to drive in an expanding circle, which would crush bushes and scrub and knock down trees, until we thought we had an area large enough and safe enough for landing. Sometimes the troops could not make a landing area, and we landed on top of their Armored Personnel Carriers (APC, or just PC), perpendicular to their long axis, and we loaded the wounded right out of their top hatch into the aircraft. Sometimes we scratched the paint.

On some missions, we went to the Qui Nhon area to support the Republic of Korea Army (ROK), who was expert at using helicopters efficiently. They were serious about warfare. Certain missions involved evacuating ARVN dead from "hot" (under fire) landing zones. Some of these bodies had been in body bags for days in the sun. The Vietnamese pilots would not evacuate their dead themselves because they were superstitious. After being assigned to do this chore several times, I found myself becoming superstitious, mostly about someone shooting at me while I did someone else's work. I was not fond of this mission, but I chalked it up to just another hazard of combat.

Other missions I ran might be a combat assault involving all the 189th lift ships or a larger assault involving multiple assault helicopter companies. One assault in particular near Dak To was comprised of about 80 lift ships covered by several dozen gunships. These missions were always exciting yet dangerous since we, by nature, were assaulting NVA formations. They were experienced in helicopter warfare. They knew what to expect, and there were losses.

This sign identifies the parent unit at Camp Holloway, which controls all the aviation assets located there.

(Above) These are the medals the author received for his service in Vietnam. Top row: Army Aviator Wings; Second row: The Air Medal with "V" Device for valor, the Air Medal with 2nd through 30th Oak Leaf Cluster for "meritorious achievement while participating in aerial flight," the Army Commendation Medal for meritorious service; Third row: The Purple Heart for "wounds received in action," the Good Conduct Medal, the National Defense Service Medal, the Vietnam Service Medal with two bronze stars, and the Vietnam Campaign Medal.

(Below) The crosses represent aircraft lost by the 189th. Each cross carries the tail serial number of a specific ship. "Ghostriders" had "Caretakers." In this case, the Caretakers were our maintenance crew, the 604th Transportation Detachment. The Caretakers did their level best to keep our combat-damaged aircraft airworthy. The unit insignia, from left to right, are 189th Assault Helicopter Company "Ghostriders," 1st Aviation Brigade (who controlled all aviation assets in Vietnam), 52nd Combat Aviation Battalion "Flying Dragons," and the 604th Transportation Detachment.

(Above) *30 May 1968.* I leave my hooch as "Ghostrider 22." In a lift ship or "slick," pilots sought a higher level of personal protection. In this case, I not only wore chest armor plate, but I also donned a "flak jacket." I found that the chest armor deflected rounds, which came up from below into the pilot's face. This circumstance was not a happy one. The flak jacket was designed to prevent this deflection from happening. The jacket absorbed ricochets and fragments as they bounced off the chest armor plate. My large, black RON bag contained a survival kit, C-rations, canteen, camera, and other combat necessities. As a Ghostrider, I also carried a Colt M1911A1 .45 caliber automatic. A Special Forces sergeant pointed out to me that I could still load, cock, and fire this weapon if I ever lost or disabled an arm or hand, which was a major consideration for combat air crews. I could not do the same with a .38 caliber revolver. "Besides," the sergeant said when comparing the relative firepower of the two weapons, "You want to knock 'em down, not just piss 'em off!" I took the sergeant's advice.

(Below) *15 May 1968.* This building is the "den" for the "Flying Dragons," complete with a bar. The Officer's Club at Camp Holloway was a sanctuary that saved the sanity of all who walked inside it. Within the club's nether regions, we found cool drinks, hot food, slot machines, poker tables, music, laughter, and best of all, comradeship. This club was a very necessary place to decompress.

Citation

BY DIRECTION OF

THE SECRETARY OF THE ARMY

The Army Commendation Medal

(FIRST OAK LEAF CLUSTER)
IS PRESENTED TO

CHIEF WARRANT OFFICER CW2 ROBERT N. STEINBRUNN W3155719
UNITED STATES ARMY

who distinguished himself by exceptionally meritorious service in support of military operations against communist aggression in the Republic of Vietnam. During the period

OCTOBER 1967 TO OCTOBER 1968

he astutely surmounted extremely adverse conditions to obtain consistently superior results. Through diligence and determination he invariably accomplished every task with dispatch and efficiency. His unrelenting loyalty, initiative and perseverance brought him wide acclaim and inspired others to strive for maximum achievement. Selflessly working long and arduous hours, he has contributed significantly to the success of the allied effort. His commendable performance was in keeping with the finest traditions of the military service and reflects distinct credit upon himself and the United States Army.

PPC-Japan

(Above) These official orders award the author with the Army Commendation Medal for meritorious service when he served with the 189th Helicopter Assault Company.

(Above) The air traffic radar control unit (Pleiku Center) at the airfield at Camp Holloway. Living under the threat of NVA mortar and rocket attack is a way of life for those based at this Highland oasis.

(Below) *30 May 1968.* GIs from time immemorial have a sardonic sense of humor as indicated by this sign. Perhaps their humor allows them to keep their sanity and to survive.

(Below) *30 May 1968.* Camp Holloway's pilot hooches had four rooms with two pilots to a room. Each hooch had a central common area for a bar, table, and refrigerator. These hooches have sandbagged lower walls to contain mortar fragments. We either hit the deck or rolled into our underground bunker if mortars struck.

(Above) Our hooch area next to the perimeter wire at Camp Holloway shows an APC patrolling the road to Pleiku that runs by on the outside of the wire. Occasionally, pilots received orders to defend the perimeter segment. By that time, we had M16 assault rifles and felt a bit more confident about our weaponry.

(Below) *Camp Holloway Airfield, 30 May 1968.* Many of our aircraft are being patched up, inspected, and test flown in the maintenance hangars. The ramp and runway were overlaid with Pierced Steel Planking (PSP) that not only provided a stable landing surface but also kept the mud and dust to a minimum. The PSP was a little tricky to land on when wet, but a pilot could not have everything. The yellow circle in the left foreground marked the "hot spot" where we parked our H-models when we had nighttime flare ship duty. When the NVA launched mortar or rocket attacks, we scrambled to get airborne from this spot so we could orbit the perimeter at about 4,000 feet. We then dropped magnesium parachute flares upon any request from units that manned the guard posts and that wanted more illumination.

(Above) *31 May 1968.* A new mount, a Bell UH-1H, which is a long-cabin Huey with the more powerful Lycoming T53-L-13 gas turbine engine of 1,400 shp. This helicopter was the Company Commander's personal ship (highly waxed) but was assigned to me due to combat losses that caused a shortage of aircraft. The machine gun mount received its M60 prior to a mission.

(Below) *31 May 1968.* The Company Commander's ship carries a zig-zag, single-side band radio antenna along the side of the tail boom. The 189th, comprised of the Silver and Scarlet Lift Platoons, was represented by the stylized silver and scarlet "S" letters on the tail fin.

(Above) Bell UH-1H of the 189th AHC has "189" painted on each pilot door in black. All units in the 52nd CAB have their company number painted on the side of the ship as an identification marking.

(Below) The cargo compartment door slides aft on tracks, and a smaller door hinges forward for cabin access. The door gunners sit in the rear and face outward behind their M60 guns. The door gunners enjoy a grand view.

(Top Right) The UH-1H is powered by the Lycoming T53-L-13 turbine engine. The cowlings swing aside to allow excellent access to everything.

(Top Left) The copilot sits on the left. Both pilots have armor seats with a sliding armor plate, which locks into position for side protection once the pilot is buckled in. The seat belt buckle feeds through the shoulder harness end loops and locks everything in place with a quick-release lever. The copilot's collective pitch (up and down lever) and cyclic (joy stick) can be seen. The red handles underneath this seat to the rear allow the door gunner to unlock the seat and hinge it aft and down to extract a wounded (or worse) pilot from the cockpit. Standard operating procedure (SOP) requires a pilot to lock his shoulder harness before flying into a hot area. If a pilot is hit, he will not lurch forward onto the flight controls, which could make a bad situation even worse. The Huey has two windshield wipers, but the monsoon rains easily make a mockery of their effectiveness. To the top right, a map light and its coiled cord dangle in the pilot's overhead tinted window. The overhead console contains switches and knobs for the battery, generator, position lights, rotating beacon, circuit breakers, windshield wipers, pitot heat, and other ancillary equipment. The control pedestal between the pilots contains engine and fuel controls and all of the communication and navigation radios needed for limited instrument flight rules (IFR) flying.

(Bottom) The aft cabin has emergency exits in the doors, which are of little use since we fly with the doors open.

2 June 1968. **A 189th AHC UH-1H has its windshield cleaned by the crew chief before a morning flight.**

What Ghostriders Do All Day

The majority of our missions were flown single-ship, much like delivery trucks on call, and we only seemed to fly in company strength during combat assaults. Other varied missions are illustrated by excerpts from my pilot's log book, which reflect actual daily experiences that were common to us:

- "RON at The Pit" (Dak To, a not-nice neighborhood).
- "Shooting pinnacles (mountaintop approaches) into many fire bases at Dak To."
- "Flying Visual Recons (VR), sling loads, landing on pad on a slope on the side of a mountain."
- "Inserted Long Range Reconnaissance Patrol (LRRP) team to blow bridge the NVA have been using for truck traffic."
- "After dark ammo resupply to fire base with no lights of any kind (aircraft or ground) due to attracting NVA mortar fire."
- "Engine dirty, had compressor stall, aircraft grounded."
- "Made dusk extraction of Hawkeye team who were under fire, heard automatic weapons fire on their radio, they piled on board laughing and shooting down at NVA pursuers. Some game! Go play somewhere else!"
- "Flew flare ship at 0200, dropped flares around Holloway perimeter, NVA sappers infiltrating to destroy aircraft."
- "Practice on McGuire Rescue Rig." (Four 100 ft. nylon straps attached to the cargo tie-down rings in the cabin. These straps hung below the aircraft. Used to extract troops from jungle where no LZ was present.)
- "Flew 20 klicks into Laos on Hatchet team extraction."
- "Caribou smashed in due to rain. Flew CBS TV team to this and other hot spots."
- "Shot through engine, lost all oil. $60,000 turbine gone."
- "Landed on Leghorn, small pad on sheer cliff deep in Laos."
- "Flew Brigade CO on recon west of Dak To. Saw smoke from NVA firing rockets at Fire base 29 (FB29). He called in accurate artillery. End of problem."
- "Inserted three ARVNs in NVA uniforms as agents in Laos."
- "Had first ride suspended 100 feet below helicopter in McGuire Rig." (Required before flying troops in this.)
- "Extracted half of agent team in NVA uniforms in hot LZ, other agent and prisoner were temporarily spotted, not seen again for extraction."
- "Other agent found, he had killed his prisoner, was then brought home."
- "Tried to extract team in deep trouble, chopped bamboo trees in too-tight LZ, couldn't get in, aircraft got shot four times, one American left in LZ."
- "Ammo box tore loose from gunner's mount. smashed synchronized elevator."
- "Climbed to 15,000 feet to get over IFR mountains. Cold."
- "Searched for overdue and downed OH-13. Found ship crashed, two bodies burned in wreckage. Paymaster on board, millions of dollars in Military Payment Certificates (MPC) scattered around area."
- "Flew along coast by Nha Trang. Rugged rocks, French lighthouse, beautiful South China Sea."
- "Attained height of 17,000 feet due to NVA flak."
- "Climbed to max altitude of 18,000 feet due to flak."
- "Had ARVN leap out of ship at 15 feet above LZ."

(Above) The door gunner scans the river below for NVA.

(Below) Several 189th AHC aircraft sit on an airstrip listening to the FM radio prior to a combat assault.

The pilot sits on the right of the UH-1H's instrument panel. His collective pitch lever is to his left.

Forward Operating Base II Mission

The United States Army Special Forces (SF) had a number of Forward Operating Bases (FOB) in Vietnam, one of which was north of Pleiku, just south of Kontum. FOB II and the missions staged out of there were the stuff of legend and storybooks. The SF required aviation support for most of these hair-raising adventures, which meant calling upon the 52nd CAB for helicopters. This FOB II mission would rotate among the various companies within the battalion to spread the risk around, and every few months the 189th AHC had its turn to fly with the Green Berets for about 30 days straight. Much of what was done was clandestine and only oblique references are made to this time in various publications today. To those of us involved, these missions seemed larger than life. They were unreal, risky, and very effective. The worst sort of pulp fiction might come inadvertently close to what was done in this area where Vietnam, Laos, and Cambodia share a common border, but little of these missions ever made the press.

We flew in company strength, which meant both the Silver and the Scarlet Lift Platoons went together. The flight took approximately 30-minutes from Camp Holloway north to FOB II. Here, we landed, shut down, and attended a briefing on the day's activities. We might have to insert SF "A" Teams into Laos, which often meant landing in a bomb crater to drop them off at a hover. We might insert NVA defectors back into their own territory to stir up trouble among their original units.

At that time, a "Chieu Hoi" or "Open Arms" program existed to encourage defections among the enemy, and millions of leaflets were dropped over known NVA positions (we conducted these drops too) to provide them with information on how to defect. Each leaflet contained a paper pass. I was never very comfortable looking back over my armor seat at a cabin full of Vietnamese in NVA uniforms with Russian or Chinese automatic weapons. I knew I was landing them among their former friends. I never knew where their loyalties might lie once we arrived or what changes of heart might occur.

Sometimes we dropped off Long Range Reconnaissance Patrols (LRRP), who scouted out NVA positions, captured prisoners, and required pickup or "extraction" a week or so later, or sooner, if they were pursued by NVA units. Invariably, these extractions were suspenseful, minute-by-minute missions that involved rapid changes of plans, air strikes from supporting A-1s directed by an FAC in a Cessna O-2, and suppressive fire laid down by our own gunships as we went into hot LZs. The entire area was comprised of rugged mountains and karst, and often the only landing zones available were bomb craters left over from an "Arc Light," a B-52 strike. We usually could not touch down in a bomb crater, but we could hover low enough to drop off or embark troops.

If we could not hover low enough, we used a McGuire Rig. This rescue rig consisted of four nylon straps, each 100 feet long, each with a loop at the bottom for someone to sit in or thread under their arms. The upper end of the straps snapped into the cargo tie-down rings in the aft cabin floor of the Huey. When needed, the coiled straps were tossed out the doors, two per side, and the pilot maneuvered the loop ends below into the pickup zone to the waiting troops. Sometimes, our door gunners guided us down on the intercom system (ICS) of the aircraft. Sometimes the grunts below talked us down on the radio. When all four "passengers" were nestled in their strap loops, we lifted them vertically upwards until they cleared the trees. The troops dangled below the ship at 80 knots because we had no way to winch them aboard. They dangled as we flew them back to a safe landing area where we could touch them down, land, and load them aboard the helicopter. This operation might involve 30 minutes to an hour of flight time spent dangling.

I took a familiarization ride in the McGuire Rig before I was allowed to fly anyone in it, and I can attest to the "excitement" and "adventure" involved in extended flight below a helicopter. We wondered how much chafe the straps could stand, and we flew at a slow 80 knots so the troops' field gear was not ripped off by the wind.

Special Forces Operating Base (FOB) II, Kuntum, 7 June 1968. This area is the helicopter staging area.

DEPARTMENT OF THE ARMY
HEADQUARTERS 1ST AVIATION BRIGADE
APO San Francisco 96384

GENERAL ORDERS
NUMBER 5950

"NGUY HEIM"

29 August 1968

AWARD OF THE AIR MEDAL FOR HEROISM

1. TC 320. The following AWARDS are announced.

Awarded: Air Medal (First Oak Leaf Cluster) with "V" Device
Date action: 13 June 1968
Theater: Republic of Vietnam
Reason: For heroism while engaged in aerial flight in connection with military operations against a hostile force: These men distinguished themselves by exceptionally valorous actions while serving as pilots of troop carrying helicopters participating in the rescue of a friendly ground unit west of Dak To. As their helicopters approached the landing zone, they began receiving heavy enemy automatic weapons fire. Subsequent strikes by Air Force "Skyraiders" failed to decrease the concentrated fire prior to their approach. The supporting helicopter gunships made firing passes which also failed to suppress enemy fire or cover the helicopters' approach. In the midst of peril, these men braved heavy enemy fire and directed their crews to return fire. They handled all radio traffice and assisted their aircraft commanders. They performed with noble valor under horrendous conditions and contributed immensely to the success of the mission. Their actions were in keeping with the highest traditions of the military service and reflect great credit upon themselves, their unit, and the United States Army.
Authority: By direction of the President under the provisions of Executive Order 9158, 11 May 1942, as amended by Executive Order 9242-A, 11 September 1942 and United States Army Vietnam Message 16695 dated 1 July 1966.

ALBRECHT, STANLEY B. 05244128 SSAN: ████████ FIRST LIEUTENANT
TRANSPORTATION CORPS, United States Army, 189th Aslt Hel Co, APO 96318
BRADSHAW, DANIEL L. 05538800 SSAN: ████████ FIRST LIEUTENANT
TRANSPORTATION CORPS, United States Army, 189th Aslt Hel Co, APO 96318
HALLER, WILLIAM C. W3160055 SSAN: ████████ WARRANT OFFICER W1
United States Army, 189th Aslt Hel Co, APO 96318
STEINBRUNN, ROBERT N. W3155719 SSAN: ████████ CHIEF WARRANT OFFICER CW2
United States Army, 189th Aslt Hel Co, APO 96318

FOR THE COMMANDER:

DONALD E. MULLIGAN
LTC, Artillery
Chief of Staff

OFFICIAL:

LEE S. PETERSON
1LT, AGC
Asst Adjutant General

The author was awarded the Air Medal with "V" Device for valor during actions that occurred on 13 June 1968. The text of these orders describes what he did.

(Top) *7 June 1968.* ARVN Military Police (MP) scrutinize American pilots passing through the gate at FOB II. Some of the armed indigenous troops wear uniforms with no insignia at all. They could be ARVN, Regional Forces/Popular Forces (RFPF or "rough puffs"), Hmong mercenaries, Montagnards, or NVA. All of the FOB II missions I flew were briefed, coordinated, and controlled by a Special Forces sergeant E-7, who had unusual authority for an enlisted man in the U.S. Army, but not for the Special Forces. I never saw a Special Forces commissioned officer at any of these events.

(Bottom Left) *7 June 1968.* The road outside the FOB II gate carries varied traffic such as a customized civilian tow truck with an A-frame on the front end for lifting, an M151 loaded with gear, a bicycle, and a civilian bus heading north to Kontum.

(Bottom Right) *7 June 1968.* Local mechanics at FOB II refurbish an armored car left by the French, a GM of Canada C15TA 4x4, in the hopes of having their own organic armor. Some unusual and operative vehicle improvisations were found in the field.

(Bottom Left) *7 June 1968*. Two of the many "unknowns" ready to be flown into a Laotian LZ. One carries the long M16; the other one carries the shorter CAR-15.

(Top) *7 June 1968*. Three 189th AHC H-model lift ships fly ahead for Laos and an uncertain welcome. The door gunners expect trouble and man their M60s.

(Above) An Asiatic Black Bear kept as a pet at FOB II loves grape soda pop and easily opens the can. He gets all the pop he wants since every passing troop wants to see him drink. The bear is happy to oblige passersby.

(Below) The Colt Automatic Rifle Model 15 (CAR-15) is a shorter version of the M16 and comes with a sliding stock.

Dozens of artillery fire bases were situated on the tops of mountains surrounding Dak To and west of Kontum. These fire bases provided fire support to troops, SF teams, and mechanized cavalry units that operated on the valley floors below. Creating a fire base was a sophisticated undertaking. A pioneer unit rappelled down from a hovering helicopter with chain saws and supporting infantry. They clear-cut an LZ that would accommodate a Huey so it could bring heavier equipment and covering troops. Then, a Crane sling-loaded a bulldozer and then its tracks. This equipment cleared mountaintops, established fields of fire, dug bunkers, and erected defensive positions. The NVA hated these fire bases since the 105 mm howitzers could send a greeting 11,160 meters, which is almost 7 miles.

When a number of fire bases with interlocking fields of fire were established, our troops could control a wide area. The fire bases needed good defenses since they represented prime targets themselves. The troops at the fire bases also needed supplies, hot meals in cans, ammunition, replacement troops, concertina wire, and many other essentials. Helicopters were the only vehicle that could ferry all these supplies, and these types of flights represented a great deal of our flying in the Central Highlands.

That a replacement GI was flown into a fire base, spent his entire tour of duty on that hill, and was flown out one year later was a difficult concept for me to grasp. When I flew new replacements into the fire base, they looked crestfallen at what they saw. When I flew the short-timers out, the ones who were going back to the states, they often looked like haunted men. Occasionally, I looked back in the cabin at them after I cleared the mountain. I saw several faces wet from tears. At times like these, I felt I was doing something very special.

(Above) I approach a fire base with mail and a load of "hots" or hot meals in large thermal cans for the artillerymen. The flight helmet I wear is an APH-5. My patch is that of the 1st Aviation Brigade.

(Below) *2 July 1968.* On final approach to a fire base west of Dak To, I see the purple smoke grenade that marks the LZ. The clearing at the bottom is for sling loads delivered by the "heavies." The 105s are covered with canvas tarps.

(Above) On a short final approach to the fire base landing pad, I see the dozer has done an effective job clearing the hill.

(Below) As our aircraft decelerates, we see troops who will unload the aircraft and reload it with all the items on the ground, which include the red bags seen here.

(Above) This sandbagged bunker next to the landing pad is part of the perimeter defense. 105s can reach out 7 miles.

(Below) Supplies are unloaded out the left cabin door. The 105 mm howitzers sit in their emplacements. This place is clearly a rugged area to live and work. It is not a safe neighborhood in the first place.

Flying ARVN Artillery VIPs to Nha Trang

On 3 July 1968, I received only one mission sheet, which was unusual. However, the mission required a full day and was a dream mission. My orders required me to fly to Camp Holloway with an ARVN Lt. Colonel and his staff to inspect an ARVN artillery encampment near Ban Me Thuot. Then, I needed to fly them southeast to the coastal city of Nha Trang. This assignment promised to be one of the more scenic flights I would experience. I was glad I brought my camera.

I loaded and briefed our passengers. They were courteous and spoke English. I knew this day would be a special one where I was glad to be alive and doing the work I did. The sky was blue. The sun was warm but not hot. Even Vietnam seemed at its most colorful. After the brief stopover at the artillery encampment, I headed southeast for Nha Trang, and I saw some of the most vivid coastal scenery in Vietnam.

(Above) The ARVN artillery encampment is ringed with concertina wire with tin cans tied to it as an alarm system. The Republic of South Vietnam flag flies proudly at the flagpole. The flag is yellow with three horizontal red stripes.

(Below) The VIPs prepare to board the aircraft for the next leg. The letter "H" denotes a helipad and is made up of white-painted sandbags.

(Top) Outside the perimeter concertina wire, an ARVN troop's family plays in the tropical vegetation. Partial ruins of a Buddhist monastery lie behind them. The Annamite Mountains stand in the distance.

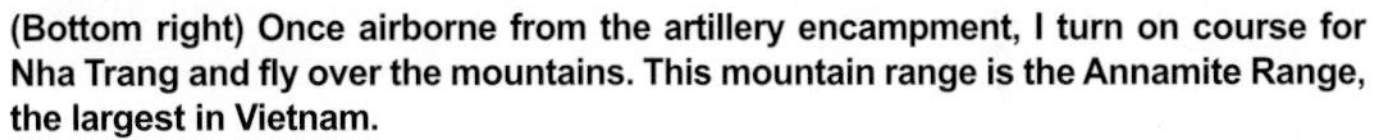

(Bottom right) Once airborne from the artillery encampment, I turn on course for Nha Trang and fly over the mountains. This mountain range is the Annamite Range, the largest in Vietnam.

(Bottom left) This guard tower forms the perimeter defense at the ARVN encampment. The tower looks well-protected with its sandbags and automatic weapons. The guards do not like having their photo taken or having me so close to them.

(Above) *3 July 1968.* After we arrive safely at the ARVN compound in Nha Trang, our passengers bid us farewell. I am impressed with the ingenuity of the hot shower to the right rear, which is a drop tank, stolen from the Air Force, that holds water warmed by an immersion heater.

(Above) Holding ponds harvesting salt from the sea appear geometric and well-tended while levels of terraced rice paddies climb the slope of the mountains.

(Below) A peninsula juts out into the South China Sea, which is catching the surf. The beaches are virtually deserted.

(Above) This scenic fishing village is vertically below us, about 4,000 feet.

(Below) An old French lighthouse perches majestically on a sheer cliff and reflects the late afternoon sun.

Medevac for Ambushed Convoy

The 189th AHC was not a dedicated "Dustoff" Medical Evacuation (medevac) unit, but wounded GIs had priority over anything else. Consequently, we frequently found ourselves diverted by radio from our assigned mission and sent to pick up wounded troops. We received the requesting unit's call sign and the tactical FM radio frequency for contacting them. Then, we had the ability to find them using the FM Homing equipment installed in the Huey. If the LZ was safe enough, we landed, loaded, and left without ever shutting down our aircraft. We then flew the wounded to the 71st Evacuation Hospital in Pleiku. From initial pickup to landing on the helipad by the 71st Evac, we took seldom more than an hour in our Area of Operations.

Being part of this life-saving procedure was one of the most rewarding aspects of flying helicopters in Vietnam. We never got to know any of those we carried in these circumstances, but often we looked back at them on the cabin floor and received a weak grin, a hint of a smile, or even a "thumbs up." My regard for the Army went up several notches because of the priority it assigned to the wounded. I was glad to be a part of it.

On 11 July 1968, we were flying a resupply mission when we received one of these calls from our operations section. A convoy on the highway between Kontum and Dak To was ambushed by NVA units and had several wounded. We were the closest ship and were diverted to the unit, which we easily found by using the FM homing procedure once we established radio contact with them. This ambush was "hit-and-run," and the NVA melted away into the jungle by the time we arrived. We deemed the area safe enough to land on the muddy road by a "deuce and a half" gun truck mounting an M2HB .50 caliber Browning machine gun. An ACAV guarded the other side of our aircraft while we loaded the wounded GI. I was a bit surprised to see he had been shot in the "tail boom," to use aviation vernacular, and he was placed prone on the cabin floor. Turning to me, the GI managed a weak grin and gave me a "thumbs up." He had the "million-dollar" wound, and he knew it. His injury was serious enough for him to get medevac'd out of Vietnam, but not serious enough to be disabling. We had him on the pad by the 71st Evacuation Hospital in Pleiku in about 30 minutes. After observing where he was wounded, we felt even more grateful for our armored seats.

An M113 Armored Cavalry Assault Vehicle (ACAV) covers our helicopter as we hover over a muddy road to pick up wounded GIs. The infantry fanned out into the edge of the jungle in pursuit of the NVA, who ambushed the convoy. Maximum firepower was directed at the tree line.

(Above) An M35A1 "deuce and a half" (2 ½ ton useful load) gun truck covers us while we load our casualty. Their .50 caliber Browning means business. They must not have much fun living and working in the mud.

(Below) From the evacuation hospital, more serious injuries might be transferred to a larger rear echelon hospital like this one near Qui Nhon. Despite being in a rear area, they still need bunkers.

The wounded cavalryman has a field dressing on his "tail boom" and lays on the cabin floor with a weak grin and a "thumbs up." We have him back at the 71st Evacuation Hospital in 30 minutes. He's going home.

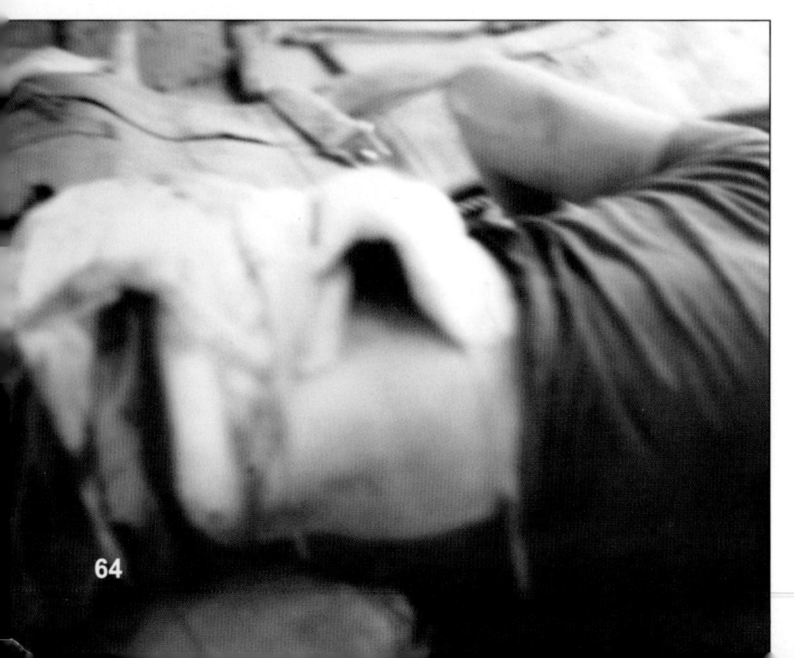

Several more excerpts from my pilot's logbook illustrate that any helicopter could become a medevac ship, not just the dedicated "Dustoff" Medical Evacuation units. The situation all depended on who was closest and what that person was doing at the moment. The Army deserves a lot of credit for its approach of taking care of its wounded. I felt gratified to be part of the system. We got to know the helipad at the 71st Evacuation Hospital in Pleiku all too well.

- "Combat assault on 2 NVA companies, GI KIA by rocket."
- "7/17 Cav slick shot to pieces at Duc Lap. Track unit (mechanized cavalry) had contact, medevac'd 5 GIs, 3 serious, 1 shot in groin. After medevac we put in combat assault blocking force."
- "Went into hot LZ to pick up dead + wounded ARVNs. Lt. Colonel wrote crew up for awards. Best one is surviving."
- "Did visual recon, LRRP insertion, GI extraction. #263 got shot up badly, brought pilots home."
- "CH-47 hit by 37 mm explosive round, nice hole. No injuries requiring medevac.

Special Forces Camp: Plei Mrong

The United States Army Special Forces (Green Berets) established numerous strategic hamlets and training camps throughout Vietnam, many of which became famous. One camp in particular was written about extensively and figured prominently in the lives of 189th AHC pilots. This camp was Plei Mrong, located about 23 klicks northwest of Pleiku and 26 klicks southwest of Kontum. The camp was situated several klicks west of Highway 14 on a narrow plain that formed a natural conduit for NVA units that moved into the Pleiku area from the Ho Chi Minh trail. The Special Forces were established there to watch this traffic, report on it, and do what they could to harass it.

Artillery was sited to provide interdiction and fire support to units operating there, and "Spooky" AC-47 gunships from Pleiku Airbase could reach the area on short notice. AC-47s dispensed awesome and gruesome firepower. Helicopter gunships from the 52nd CAB knew the area well. Our own 189th AHC UH-1Cs, the "Avengers," were part of the CAB.

Brief internet searches turn up accounts of battles in the area, after-action reports, memorandums to the President, and other pieces of information revealing how strategic a hamlet this place was and the many hair-raising adventures American forces had in this area. We were not fond of going there.

I look serious as I hold two projectiles removed from NVA troops killed in action (KIA) at Plei Mrong. The projectile on the left is a 57 mm recoilless rife round that has a range of over 4,000 meters and fires from a weapon served by a crew of three. The projectile on the right is a rocket propelled grenade for an RPG-7 shoulder-fired tube launcher. The RPG-7 has a range of 500 meters and is effective against personnel, armor, and especially helicopters. Both projectiles have Chinese lettering and markings.

With my fellow pilot Paul Stoddard, I discuss the imminent combat assault on NVA forces located northwest of Plei Mrong. The M60 machine gun is scrutinized to ensure it is clean, oiled, and has plenty of 7.62 mm ammo. The M60 is the UH-1H lift ship's friend. These two door guns are the only real weapons we have. Several smoke grenades are tied to the seat post. The door gunner uses the grenades to mark targets or areas where we receive fire for the gunships, artillery, or Tactical Air (TacAir) fighter bombers. Watching napalm hit is like looking at Hell.

(Above) 25 August 1968. My ship, 67-17272, has new markings. "Barbie" (my girlfriend) now appears on the nose. A yellow "272" appears on the fin. Red and white stripes identify the 52nd CAB and encircle the tail boom. The tail rotor is Olive Drab with yellow tips instead of black with red and white stripes.

(Below) We are about 1,000 feet in the air above the Special Forces camp at Plei Mrong during our circling approach to landing. We will spiral tightly down over the camp to avoid receiving fire from the tree lines. One of our ships is already shut down on the helipad and awaiting the rest of us. The camp has several rings of concertina wire around it, defensive fire posts and bunkers connected by a trench network, and a "last ditch" citadel.

(Above) This village is located outside Plei Mrong and is home to the Degar people or "Montagnards" (mountain people), as the French called them. These people are indigenous to the Central Highlands. Their homes are elevated above predatory animals, reptiles, and insects, and are clean and orderly. The various tribes of Degar (Jarai, Rhade, Bahnar, Koho, Mnong, and Stieng) have many of their men fighting with the Special Forces. They are formidable warriors.

(Below) *Plei, Mrong, 25 August 1968.* Women and children of the Jarai tribe of Degar people (Montagnards) pose for the camera by one of the woven bamboo sheds that contains firewood. One woman smokes marijuana wrapped in a banana leaf, which is an ancient tribal custom and an inexpensive form of relaxation for these people. They grow both the banana leaves and the marijuana.

Pleiku Airbase. This AC-47 "Spooky" gunship of the 4th Air Commando Squadron (tail code EN) provides fire support for besieged Special Forces camps such as Plei Mrong. The aircraft is painted in standard USAF Southeast Asia camouflage with gloss black undersurfaces and with a spectral ghost on the nose. The Spooky carried a crew of eight that consisted of the pilot, copilot, navigator, flight engineer, load master, two gunners, and usually a South Vietnamese observer. GIs called the aircraft "Puff the Magic Dragon" after a song popular at the time. These aircraft are extremely effective at sealing off camps from attackers. The Spooky flies at a leisurely 120 knots in a circle to the left. The pilot observes his target through a side-mounted gun sight. On 8 February 1965, a Spooky over the Bong Son plain decimated a Viet Cong (VC) attack. The Spooky loitered and fired for over four hours. An estimated 20,500 rounds were fired into the enemy position. More than 300 VC troops were killed. Weapons like these were responsible for the disparity in casualty figures during the Vietnam war. U.S. government statistics show more than 58,200 American servicemen and women were killed in the conflict while the Vietnamese government gives the number of their troops killed in action as a staggering 1,100,000.

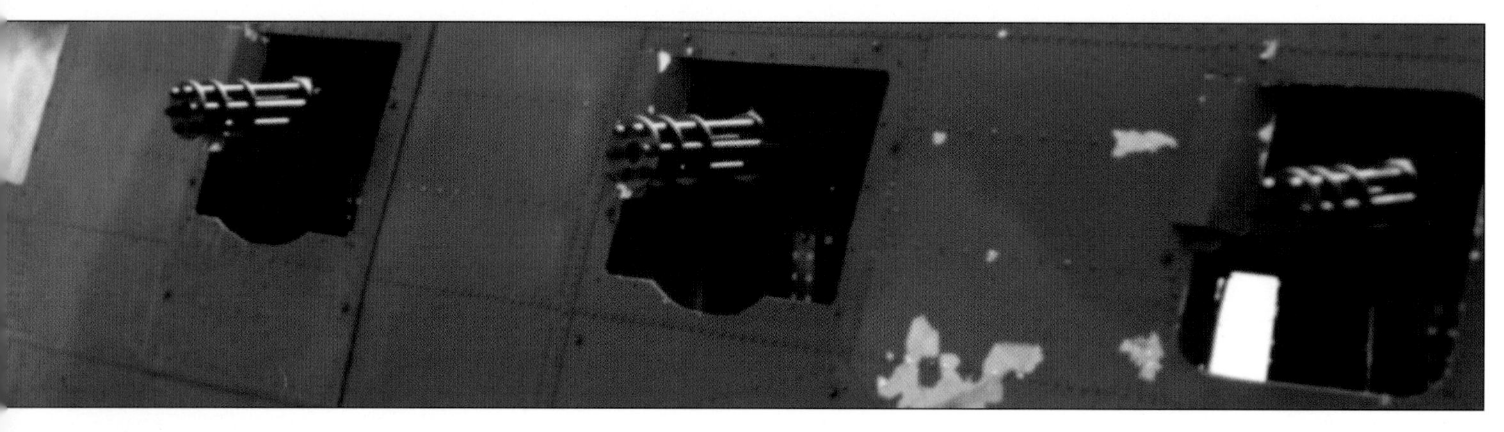

(Above) Three General Electric GAU-2B/A 7.62 mm Miniguns comprise the main armament of the AC-47. The aircraft can carry 45 magnesium parachute flares and 54,000 rounds of ammunition, which is enough for about three minutes at the full rate of fire. Seeing these weapons belching flames from the ground at night and hearing their noise is quite an experience.

(Below) *25 August 1968.* I look rumpled but relieved as I leave Plei Mrong with my aircraft. I leave in the rain and head back for Camp Holloway. The pilot's sliding window is open a bit for air circulation to prevent the plexiglass from fogging. The 52nd CAB has ordered the unit numbers removed from all aircraft at this point, but vestiges of it remain on the door.

Siege and Relief: Duc Lap Special Forces Camp

On 25 August 1968, the NVA attacked the Special Forces camp at Duc Lap, southwest of Ban Me Thuot and close to the Cambodian border. A three-day battle ensued. After breaching the perimeter wire, the NVA overran the camp. Special Forces, Mike Forces, and Civilian Irregular Defense Group (CIDG) troops counterattacked the camp with the help of helicopter gunships and AC-47 Spooky gunships out of Pleiku Airbase. After an epic struggle, the camp was retaken. A body count turned up more than 303 dead NVA soldiers. This camp figured prominently in the news in 1975, when the NVA staged a second attempt at capture. This time, they committed over 4,000 regular troops to the battle. By cutting the defenders off from the camp's vital airstrip, the NVA were able to capture it. These bloody events are recounted in the 1999 book *Through the Wire*. On 15 September 1968, we were sent to Duc Lap on a combat assault against NVA forces still in the area. We staged from the Duc Lap airstrip and flew troops to several LZs in the area. Despite having lost the battle, the NVA were still a formidable and well-armed foe. They fought tenaciously and did not easily give up.

***15 September 1968.* A CH-47 Chinook or "hook" delivers a sling load of ammunition to Duc Lap. The door gunner watches from behind his M60 machine gun where he appears to maintain a firm grip on it. This ship is from the 180th Assault Support Helicopter Company, call sign "Big Windy." Anyone who has unhooked a cargo net from a belly hook of a Chinook knows where the name originates. The Special Forces camp is situated on the hill and commands excellent fields of fire. Multiple rings of defensive bunkers and trenches encircle the camp while high-powered radio antennae sprout from the command post. The Chinook wobbles slightly as it touches its load down. It then hovers over to the airstrip next to us to set down. The aircraft has taken a 37 mm explosive round in the fuselage just aft of the cockpit on the right side. The crew chief has some fragments in his face, but his chest plate protects his vital organs. After inspecting the Chinook, he decides the aircraft and crew are still airworthy, and the "hook" departs for home. Duc Lap is not a nice neighborhood.**

(Above) *15 September 1968.* The "hook" lands and shuts down. It attracts the curious. The crew chief is up by the aft pylon to inspect for damage. The blackened hole from the 37 mm round is just behind the pilot's window.

(Below) The Chinook crew is luckier than the one on board this shot down aircraft outside the Duc Lap Special Forces camp by the airstrip. The aircraft is so trashed, we are unable to figure out what type of aircraft it was. Our crew chief thinks the rubble might be the remains of a Charley-model Huey. The local personnel will likely salvage what they can for bunker roofing or other utilitarian purposes. No one seems to know anything about the status of the crew in regard to injuries.

(Below) A 37 mm round exploded upon penetration and left a black power burn that dissipated most of its explosive force outside the aircraft. Fragments sprayed the crew chief's face, but he seemed okay. He appeared more concerned about his aircraft than his injuries–a stout fellow. He finds some minor damage to the radio black boxes, wiring harnesses, electronic components, and structure, but the crewmen decide the ship is flyable. The pilots agree. They declare Duc Lap inhospitable.

(Above) Further combat assaults were made in the area on a number of occasions. We crank up here at LZ Oasis, southwest of Pleiku, to insert troops into LZs around Duc Lap. The airstrip at Duc Lap was occasionally untenable due to sporadic NVA fire. Thus, the Oasis was almost as convenient. It was deemed eminently more safe.

(Below) This U.S. Army de Havilland U-1A Otter short takeoff and land (STOL) utility transport sits at the Oasis. The plane has a 600 hp. Pratt & Whitney, R-1340 engine that swings a Hamilton Standard propeller. The plane can seat 10, and the Army uses it for just about anything except a gunship. They land in little more distance than a helicopter.

The Legendary Major Fraker

When I first interviewed to join the Ghostriders, I met with the commanding officer of the 189th AHC, Major William W. Fraker. After moving into my hooch and meeting some of my fellow pilots, I found they were curious to know how my interview went. I replied that he was pleasant, low key, and very personable.

"What?" They cried. "Wild Bill? You gotta be kidding! Not Wild Bill!"

I assured them that I spoke the truth. I asked where he got the name "Wild Bill."

"I don't know where the name came from, but we all call him that. You can call him that, too. Anytime. It might be better, though, if you didn't call him that to his face," one pilot said.

Another pilot told me I would find out how Wild Bill got his name at the company meeting in the mess hall that night.

"You have company meetings? The entire company?" I asked.

"No, just the pilots." yet another pilot voiced, "He likes to talk to us, *special*-like."

This news sounded a bit strange to me, but no one offered further information.

"Just be there, you'll see, and bring pencil and paper with you," I was told.

"Hmmmmm, we have to take notes,." Very well, I thought, I'll take notes. We must receive extensive operational data regarding tactics, units in the area, radio frequencies, call signs, free-fire zones, and flying.

That evening, we took our seats at the tables in the mess hall, and I noticed many pilots did not have notebooks. Instead, they helped themselves to paper napkins from the dispensers on the tables.

"Ten-hut!" someone shouted.

We stood as our commanding officer entered and strode to the front of the mess hall. He faced us with a scowl. He invited us to take out seats. We did. For the next hour or so, he briefed us on all the missions we had flown the past week, the after-action reports (AAR) we had turned in, and our very questionable parentage. He boomed. He vented. He gesticulated. He seemed to do some kind of dance. He waved his arms around. Wild Bill was loud. He was angry, and above all, he was very profane.

The instrument panel of the Otter is strictly "utility" but has that nice, 1950s look. These planes are faster than they appear. They have a top speed of 160 mph.

He brought up each mistake, poor decision, lapse of judgment, and disregard for safety in which we were guilty. Every third or fourth word consisted of only four letters. His language was incredible. It was illuminating. I felt like I had taken an "Increase Your Vocabulary and Word Power" course. I was learning so much. I had no idea so many four-letter words existed in the English language. In all fairness, some words were new to me. So, they easily might have been foreign.

Wild Bill went on at length, and I realized that the other pilots were scribbling on their napkins and in their notebooks while my own paper was blank. I was incredulous. I did not know what notes they were taking during this discourse, this session of berating and lambasting, this casting of aspersions on the quality of our training, powers of observation during flight, control touch, and reason for existence.

"That'll be all," Wild Bill said. He stalked off and was fuming.

"Ten-hut!" someone shouted again.

We all rose. I was open-mouthed. I was dumbfounded. I had never seen anything like this before except perhaps from my basic training drill sergeant. However, that was expected.

"Does he always talk to you like that?" I asked one of the other pilots, "I've never seen anything quite like this before!"

"Oh, sure, always," he replied. "That's just how he shows he cares."

"Yep" another opined, "He ain't really like he is, at all!"

A third pilot said that was how the good Major got our attention.

I asked about the notes and why everyone was taking notes during this lecture.

"Oh, we're not taking notes, per se," one pilot informed me. "We're just making tic marks in an attempt to keep count."

"Tic marks for what? Counting what?" I asked.

"Well, it's for the Profanity Pool."

"Profanity Pool?" I asked.

"Sure. We all throw five bucks or so into a hat, and we all try to keep count of each four-letter word he uses. It takes all of us to keep track 'cause there's so many of 'em. Afterwards, we average everyone's total. The one pilot who comes the closest wins the pot."

"I see." This man, this kind, gentle, and caring man (on the inside) was making some pilot rich every week.

The Otter has four huge, chrome exhaust pipes that would make any hot-rodder envious. An engine oil cooler intake is at the bottom of the cowling.

The NVA Brings In Their Armor

On 6 February, the North Vietnamese brought Russian-made PT-76 amphibious tanks into action for the first time in the war at Lang Vei, about 7 klicks west of Khe Sanh. These tanks later appeared at Khe Sanh and Ben Het. While American M48A3 Patton tanks were more than able to deal with the Russian tanks, having some sort of anti-armor aviation assets in-country was deemed advisable.

Huey gunships with the XM-22 weapons sub-system were first used in combat in Vietnam in 1966, primarily against bunkers. However, the appearance of NVA armor gave new impetus to the program. This system mounted six French Nord SS-11, wire-guided anti-armor missiles on external launchers. The Army gave these missiles the Air to Ground Missile, model 22 (AGM-22) designation. The missiles weighed 66 pounds each and had a range of 500 to 3,000 meters. Their warhead weighed 15 pounds, and they flew at a speed of approximately 421 mph.

The AGM-22s reeled out a wire from a spool in the base of the missile that allowed transmission of flight commands from the helicopter copilot, who used a small joystick, to the missile.

The missile's wings had no flight control surfaces, and it reacted to inputs from the pilot by vectoring the thrust from its rocket motor nozzles. The pilot or operator tracked the flight of the missile in his sight by using a flare installed in the missile's tail. The system required highly-trained operators and steady tactical circumstances, which was not always possible in combat. The Army felt the performance of this missile system under the press of the tactical conditions that prevailed in Vietnam was unsatisfactory. The AGM-22s later were replaced in the war by the TOW missile (Tube-launched, Optically tracked, Wire-guided). TOW-equipped Hueys were used with success against NVA armor during the 1972 Spring Invasion when they destroyed no fewer than 26 North Vietnamese Army PT-76 tanks.

20 September 1968. **A Bell UH-1C, with the XM-22 Weapons sub-system, hot refuels at the Dak To airstrip. This ship belongs to my old unit, the 7th Squadron, 17th Air Cavalry, which the nose marking identifies. Only the white spur is painted on the battery compartment cover, not the yellow lightning bolt. Since the markings are incomplete, this aircraft appears as if it has been rushed into action. By this date, the Charley-model should have a particle separator (air filter) installed over the engine intake. The particle separator would be visible just behind the main rotor mast. Perhaps this missing filter is another indication of the urgency of the tactical situation. An end-on photograph would have been nice, but it would have involved walking in front of the missiles, which was not wise. In 1968, NVA PT-76 tanks appeared at the Special Forces camp of Ben Het, northwest of Dak To. The tanks were within easy striking distance of this airstrip.**

The Kings of Battle

Working out in the field alongside the artillery for almost a year made me in awe of their firepower, accuracy, and effect. Artillery is called "The King of Battle," a title well-deserved. The infantry calls itself "The Queen of Battle," in deference, I think, to artillery. Grunts often depended on "arty" in Vietnam when they were overrun by the NVA. Thus, the grunts had a high regard for arty. In dire straits, grunts occasionally chose to call arty in on their own positions when everything else failed.

(Top Left) The copilot, or missile operator, sits in the left seat, common to weapons operators in all Hueys. The missile joy stick is placed to his right, and an armrest is part of the assembly since he needs a steady hand. A canted electronic control box closest to the camera is part of the missile system. The operator watches the missile in flight through an XM58 sight that magnifies the image of the missile and the flare in its tail. This observation allows him to make flight path corrections with the joy stick much more easily. The missile rotates in flight to impart spin stability and uses vectored rocket motor thrust to adjust its path to conform to commands. Since the missile spins in flight, it needs a gyroscopic platform to determine its position relative to the ground. On launching, the rocket booster motor fires for 1.2 seconds. Then, the sustainer engine fires for 20 seconds. The missiles are small. The have about a 19 ¾ inch wing span and carry a 15-pound hollow-charge, anti-armor warhead. The control pedestal between the pilots' armor seats contains two pilot audio panels, an FM tactical radio, IFF (Identification, Friend/Foe) equipment (called a transponder by civilian pilots), an ADF (Automatic Direction Finder) radio, fuel and engine governor controls, and other ancillary equipment.

(Bottom) *20 September 1968.* One of the pilots makes adjustments to the system during refueling. The missiles are painted Olive Drab with yellow noses. The rocket motor exhaust tubes are light, metallic green. The pilot wears the patch of the 1st Air Cavalry Division on his right shoulder. The patch indicates a previous combat assignment.

Normally, a Forward Observer (FO) requested an artillery fire mission on the FM tactical radio network. These FOs were trained in the art of artillery spotting and knew the various pieces, such as the M101, 105 mm howitzer, and the M107, 175 mm self-propelled gun; their ballistics, and their capabilities. FOs knew the types of shells these guns fired, where the batteries were located, and the tubes' capabilities in different types of fire missions. Additionally, FOs knew how to lay down fire and adjust it precisely. Being an FO was considered an art, and those with the title were very good at their job. We had classes in flight school on artillery spotting and direction using a large terrain board. This three-dimensional models emitted smoke from hits based on our directions, and it required practice to become good.

When not feasible for a ground FO to call in a fire mission, this airborne observers took this job and flew in Army Cessna O-1 (designated the L-19 prior to 1962) Bird Dog light airplanes. One of the most renowned units flying these diminutive warplanes in Vietnam was based at Camp Holloway. The unit was the 219th Aviation Company (Recon) "Headhunters," and their stories and achievements would fill volumes.

Camp Holloway, 22 September 1968. **Home of the 219th Aviation Company (Recon) "Headhunters."**

(Top Right) A Headhunters' pilot boards a Cessna O-1 for a mission.

(Bottom) A "Headhunters" O-1 Bird Dog sits armed and ready for its next artillery spotting mission in its revetment at Camp Holloway. Two, 2.75 inch FFAR rocket launchers are located beneath each wing. The rockets usually have 17-pound, white phosphorus warheads for marking targets. A white stripe, spanwise, on the upper surface of the wing and the horizontal stabilizers make the airplane more conspicuous to friendly (and armed) aircraft above. The "0" prefix on the aircraft's serial number, 0-12680, indicates the ship is more than 10 years-old, which means the plane is obsolete. The first prototype flew in 1949. So, the design has been part of the Army inventory for almost 20 years.

(Above) The window portion of the right-hand door swings up and latches to the wing's under surface. The door opens and latches to the wing strut. This plane is a "no-frills," business-like airplane designed for maximum visibility for a pilot and observer. The plane is powered by a six-cylinder, Continental O-470-11 engine with 190 horsepower.

(Below) The panel looks "1950-ish" because it is. To the left is the throttle quadrant with throttle, fuel mixture, propeller pitch, and carburetor air levers. The throttle has buttons for radio transmit and intercom system (ICS). The armament (rockets) control panel is the row of switches above and to the left.

All Good Things Must End

On 25 September 1968, my pilot's logbook recorded that I flew my regular aircraft from Holloway to Dak To and back again. I flew 3 hours and 35 minutes that day on resupply missions to fire bases. Upon my return to base, some engine oil leaks grounded my ship. I felt a little sad. Old 272 had been a loyal and reliable friend.

Pilots going home from the 189th AHC have a little party with those who must remain a little longer. We "short-timers" don't feel sorry for them; their DEROS will come in time. We celebrate quietly and discreetly–the only way we know how. We celebrate in the safety of our hooch, where our bunks are a few seconds crawl away. At front center, Don Wittke displays his manly chest and rubber-ringed dog tags. He thinks he makes a stealthy approach and that no one will hear him making any noise. We think he makes plenty. Clockwise to the left, I wear my M1 steel helmet with camouflage cover, which provides both concealment and protection from flying glass. I think the helmet is Don's idea. It proves to be a good one. Standing behind me is Peter Greenlaw. He wears his APH-5 flight helmet. He is ready to take flight, a wise man. In the rear, practicing escape and evasion, is Bill Haller, who wears an Australian bush hat. Jim Lomonaco sports a camouflaged beret and a manly chest while he offers a toast to those of us going home. Larry Johnson relaxes with a camo "boonie" (boondocks) hat and a "ceegar." Joe Winder wears a black beret as he slides quietly out of the picture to the right. I am not certain whether Joe makes it to his bunk. A wraith-like figure appears dimly in the doorway. It is a spectre from higher authority who admonishes us to tone down the noise. We advise him he must be mistaken. We are having a quiet and discreet party. The figure disappears silently into the murky night.

Then, something remarkable happened. The Battalion Operations officer told me I just flew my last mission. I was being stood down from further combat operations. My Date Eligible for Return Overseas (DEROS) had arrived. These words, this acronym, this "holy grail" meant the end of time in-country to troops in Vietnam. Of all the military acronyms with which we had to deal, DEROS was the one we truly embraced. My DEROS had finally come. After one year, which seemed like a lifetime, my DEROS arrived unexpectedly. Actually, several of us had reached DEROS status. We stood quietly in a group and did not know what to say. We looked at each other blankly and wondered what to do. We decided the only course open to us at this point was to have a little party.

I wrote my final remarks in my pilot's logbook on 27 September 1968:

"Finished with Vietnam. Many memories: some good, some bad, many sad. Lots of friends gone to untimely LZ in the sky. More Friends made. Hard to spend one year of your life here without leaving something of yourself behind."

***23 September 1968.* A Montagnard thatched hut carries a sign stating "Welcome To The Highlands And The 52nd Combat Aviation Battalion" at Camp Holloway airfield. This hut has some meaning for me since it's almost time to bid the 52nd CAB good-bye. My tour of duty is almost up.**

Mechanics of Returning Home

The process of going home was vastly simpler than the trip to Vietnam twelve months previously. We were trucked from Camp Holloway over to Pleiku Airbase where we were loaded on board a Fairchild C-123 Provider. This plane was a B-model and did not have the outboard jet engines of the C-123K. Hence, the plane was a bit quieter inside. Quieter meant we still could not talk at all, but at least we did not leave with a splitting headache from the jet noise. That said, no one seemed to mind the noise in the slightest. As we shuffled on board through the rear loading ramp, we saw a Kaman HH-43B Huskie rescue helicopter standing fire alert on the "hot spot" pad. Its crew watched our departure. A sign standing by the ship said, "Entry Prohibited-Alert Helicopter Cocked." Should we crash on takeoff, this twin-rotor helicopter could be airborne in one minute and would race over with a fire suppression kit slung beneath it and two rescue men, who were also firefighters, on board. The thought of crashing while leaving Vietnam after a year of everything I had experienced filled me with a sense of irony.

Several hours later, we landed at the sprawling Naval and Air base at Cam Ranh Bay. We were bussed to the transition station where we would stay overnight, have dinner at the mess hall, and then process out-of-country in the morning.

On the rain-swept apron at Pleiku Airbase, a C-123B Provider of the 310th Special Operations Wing (tail code WM) loads DEROS troops through the rear ramp.

A Kaman HH-43B Huskie on the alert pad is ready to suppress fire and rescue us if we crash during takeoff.

Part of our processing consisted of a thorough search of our persons and baggage to ensure any contraband, narcotics, weapons, or explosives were not leaving with us. I was surprised at how many of these items were found despite repeated warnings. Once clear to leave Vietnam, we had lunch and were bussed back to the airfield to board a charter flight for the States. We beheld a strange sight.

A gleaming aircraft with no trace of camouflage stood waiting for us. A flight attendant greeted us. The flight attendad was in uniform, but the uniform had no signs of the Olive Drab Color we were used to. In due course, the aircraft departed and headed eastwards for an all-night flight, which took approximately 19 hours.

Meals were served. Some troops slept. Some troops murmured quietly, read, or played cards. The quiet that filled the aircraft seemed somewhat spooky and unnatural, but every person aboard was making the mental transition back to "the real world." This transition took time and thought. All night, the flight remained quiet.

I saw that hollow, vacant "Vietnam" stare wherever I looked around the plane. In the morning, the pilots announced the cross over Washington State's coastline. Then, the troops began to stir. When we landed at McChord Air Force Base, we felt the bump from the touchdown. Then, we heard engines' reverse thrust. Suddenly, pandemonium broke out on board. Troops stood in the aisle. They hooted. They shouted. They whistled. They laughed. They threw their hats in the air. Their eyes grew wide and bright.

The troops had regained their souls.

A Chartered World Airways Boeing 707 loads DEROS troops for the flight back to the States. These guys have that vacant "Vietnam" stare.

Forty Years After Vietnam

Forty years have passed since the events I described in this book took place. I still find myself in the cockpit using the skills and lessons I learned in Vietnam. However, now I fly for humanitarian purposes, not war. I still engage in a type of medevac flying, which is now called Emergency Medical Service. The world has changed. I have changed. The aircraft have changed too. The helicopters now come with twin turbine engines, four carbon epoxy composite main rotor blades, retractable landing gear, and an autopilot with a flight director. This aircraft easily handles single-pilot Instrument Flight Rules flying and is serious high-tech medical transportation.

The flight crew has changed as well. Instead of door gunners, I fly with a critical care flight nurse and paramedic. What they know of Vietnam consists of what they have read in their history books. This crew was born long after the war ended, and Vietnam is ancient history to them. However, some things never change for me. I still get satisfaction working with dynamic, highly-trained people who make this job the closest thing to a squadron atmosphere outside the military. I still take reward in knowing I am using my skills for the benefit of others. I still get excitement from another day of flying.

After 43 years and 15,000 flight hours, I still feel the same.

(Above) I no longer wear jungle fatigues, but I still find reward in medevac.

Pronunciation Guide

- **An Khe**—ahn KAY
- **Ban Blech**—ban BLECK
- **Ban Me Thuot**—ban me TOO-it
- **Cam Rahn Bay**—CAM rahn bay
- **Camp Enari**—ee-NAHR-ee
- **Dak To**—doc TOE
- **Dong Ba Thin**—dong bah TIN
- **Duc Lap**—DUCK lap
- **Kontum**—con-TOOM
- **Lang Vei**—LANG vay
- **Nha Trang**—nah TRANG
- **Phu Cat**—FOO cat
- **Pleiku**—play KOO
- **Plei Mrong**—play merONG
- **Polei Kleng**—poly cleng
- **Khe Sanh**—KAY sahn
- **Qui Nhon**—KWEE nnyon
- **Tan Son Nhut**—tahn sahn NOOT
- **Vung Tau**—vung towel

An Agusta A-109E "Power" sits on the hospital's elevated helipad, poised for another life-saving flight.

Epilogue

The cost of war is staggering. The Vietnam War cost over an estimated $111 billion. One out of every ten servicemen and women, who served in Vietnam became a casualty, and more than 58,000[1] Americans died in the war. Was it all worth it? Many people in countries in the Pacific Rim think so. Information on common myths about the most misunderstood war in America's history and factual answers to these myths may be found on the *Vietnam Flight Crew Net* website, which is recommended by *The History Channel®*.

The Combat Area Casualty File shows one of the youngest men killed in Vietnam as 16 years of age. However, this age was not the norm, and neither was 62, the age of the oldest man killed in Vietnam The average age of a soldier kiilled in Vietnam was approximately 23.

---

1. The Combat Area Casualty File (the database that served as the basis for the Vietnam Veterans Memorial and is part of the National Archives in the Center for Electronic Records) lists 58,965 records for military personnel who died, were missing in action, or were prisoners of war as a result of the Vietnam War. Approximately 58,200 died during the war whether in combat or non-combat situations.

Specialist 5th Grade (SP5) Ronnie D. Schultz—crew chief and door gunner from Grand Junction, Colorado. Ron scans the jungle below for signs of the enemy. Ron scans the jungle below for sings of the enemy. Ron was killed in action 29 February 1968 during combat while flying in a UH-1C gunship. Ron and I served together in Alpha Troop, 7th Squadron, 17th Air Cavalry Regiment.

Warrant Officer (WO-1) Douglas A. Walker—scout pilot from Indian Orchard, Massachusetts. Doug is on small arms range at Camp Enari with .30 caliber M2 carbine and sawer-off carbine. Doug was killed in action 18 May 1968 while flying his OH-6A Loach (Cayuse). Doug and I served together in Alpha Troop, 7th Squadron, 17th Air Cavalry Regiment.

The author, now a Chief Warrant Officer (CW2), prepares to leave Cam Ranh Bay for the States in his Class A uniform. He has not worn this uniform for over a year, and it fits more loosely. The final entry in his Pilot Logbook records three words, "I made it."